Publications of the National Museum
Ethnographical Series, vol.

Deering

– a Men's house from Seward Peninsula, Alaska

By
Helge Larsen
(Edited by Martin Appelt)

Department of Ethnography
&
SILA – the Greenland Research Centre
The National Museum of Denmark
Copenhagen 2001

Deering
– a Men's house from
Seward Peninsula, Alaska
Helge Larsen and (ed. Martin Appelt)

Publications of the National Museum, vol. 19
© The National Museum of Denmark
Layout: Bent Nørregaard
Linguistic revision: Dr. Erle Nelson
Print: Special-Trykkeriet Viborg a-s

This publication can be ordered from:
Nationalmuseet
Etnografisk Samling
Frederiksholms Kanal 12
DK-1220 København K
Denmark
Phone: +45 3347 3207
Fax: +45 3347 3320
E-mail: rolf.gilberg@natmus.dk
Homepage: www.natmus.dk

ISBN: 87-89384-84-9

Contents

Editor's preface 5

List of Illustrations 8

I. Deering and the Imnachermiut 9

II. The Excavation of a House Belonging to the Ipiutak Culture 15
The Anteroom 20
Field A 22
Field B 22
Summary and Interpretation 22

III. Description of the Artifacts 27
Archery 27
  Arrowheads 27
  Arrowpoints 27
  Inset Blades 28
  Blunt Arrowheads 28
  Arrow Shafts 28
  Arrow Straightener 29
  Bows 29
  Bow guards 29
Sea mammal hunting 30
  Harpoon heads 30
  Harpoon End Blades 32
  Harpoon Socket Pieces 32
  Harpoon Foreshafts 33
Other hunting and fishing gear 33
  Lance heads 33
  Bird darts 34
  Side prongs for bird dart 35
  Throwing sticks 36
  Miscellaneous weapon shafts 36
  Snare parts 37
  Salmon spears 37
Means of Transportation 37
  Sleds 38
  Snowshoes 43
  Boats 46
  Paddles 49
Tools 49
  Wooden knife handles 49
  Flake Tools 53
  Engraving Tools 53
  Adzes 53
  Whetstones and Grinding Stones 55
  Wedges 55
  Cutting boards 55
  Mattocks and Picks 55
  Shovels 56
  Fish Scalers 57
  Two-handed scrapers 57
  Needles 57
  Awls 57
Flint Industry 57
  Flaking Tools 58

Bifaced Blades   58
Discoidal Blades   58
Unifacially Chipped Flint Implements   59
Sidescrapers   59
Other Unifacially Chipped Flint Implements   61
Household Utensils   61
  Basketry   64
  Grass Matting   64
  Spoons and ladles   64
  Fire Drills   65
Clothing and Personal Adornment   66
Art   66
Miscellaneous Objects   68

IV. References   75

Appendix A: Faunal Remains   78

Appendix B: Dating   80

Appendix C: Artifact distribution   81

Plates 1-32   82

Editor's preface

The history of the creation of the present publication has several points of departure throughout the last sixty years.

The first could be considered to have occurred in 1938 when Helge Larsen and Froelich Rainey met for the first time, at the International Congress of Anthropology and Ethnology in Copenhagen. Larsen and Rainey spoke in between sessions, and discussions soon revealed a distinct difference of opinion on the question of the origin the Eskimo culture and the settling of Arctic North America and Greenland. The two Arctic pioneers finally agreed "to settle discussions with the spade", which became Helge Larsen's "mantra" in the years to come (Larsen 1954:78).

Neither Froelich Rainey nor Helge Larsen were novices in Arctic archaeology. At the time Helge Larsen had already held a position as permanent curator at the National Museum's Ethnographic Collections for two years and was responsible for the Arctic collections. This was a position he had earned through his participation in a number of archaeological expeditions to Greenland in the 1930's: with Therkel Mathiassen in the Kangamiut District (Mathiassen 1931), on Lauge Koch's "Three Years Expedition to Northeast Greenland" (Larsen 1934), as a member of the "Mørkefjord East Greenland Expedition" (Larsen 1938) and on Lauge Koch's "East Greenland Expedition" (Koch 1940-45).

Larsen and Rainey's friendly rivalry came to a head at the village of Point Hope (*Ipiutak*) on the coast of North Alaska; a site Knud Rasmussen, after the 5th Thule Expedition, had characterized as one of the largest and most interesting sites along the Arctic shores. The discussions of disagreement that had first emerged in Copenhagen continued at Point Hope, lasted throughout the field seasons from 1939 to 1941, and in the end lead to the "construction" of the two culture historical complexes "Ipiutak" and "Near Ipiutak" (Larsen & Rainey 1948).

The fieldwork at Point Hope sparked a love of Arctic Alaska in Larsen. He was firmly convinced that the excavated material provided concrete evidence for the existence of a "palaeo-Eskimo cultural stratum" as had been suggested by Steensby (1916) and Birket-Smith (1929). Larsen also believed that the origin of the palaeo-Eskimos was to be found in the vast Alaskan inland. At a time when archaeology and ethnography were seen as closely connected it was natural for Helge Larsen to seek corroboration for his theory in the recent history of living Inuit.

He first conducted ethnographic fieldwork among the Inuit around Utorqaq (1942). In the winter of 1949 he supplemented his studies with visits to the Nunatarmiut living in the vicinity of Anaktuvuk Pass. The fieldwork was of short duration and Larsen was compelled to expand his observations. With his usual luck Larsen meet the Nunatarmiut Qarmaq and at "home" in Fairbanks met the Kangiermiut Aqsheataq (who was then 80 years old). Both men had lived most of their lives in the mountains of the interior, on the tundra and along the rivers. Helge Larsen attached great importance to these meetings and the conversations that followed; they marked his perception of Alaska's prehistory in the years to come (Larsen 1950a).

In the following years the search for the "palaeo-Eskimo cultural stratum" was again focused on doing archaeological investigations. Now in collaboration with Louis Giddings, Larsen planned and conducted investigations in Bristol Bay, Kuskowim Bay and Norton Sound respectively. This led, among other things, to Larsen's excavations at Platinum (Larsen 1950b), although these were eclipsed by Gidding's discovery of the Cape Denbigh site, which with a single stroke expanded Inuit prehistory several thousand years back in time (Giddings 1951).

In 1949 Helge devoted his attention on two tasks. The first was to locate the original site of a spectacular Ipiutak carving that had been sold to the shop in Teller the previous year. He succeeded in tracing the carving to Point Spencer, where it had been retrieved from one of three demolished Ipiutak graves. His second undertaking was to conduct excavations in the now well-known Trail Creek caves. On the way to the caves Larsen and his crew made a short stop in the village of Deering. The rest of the story can be read in Helge Larsen's own words among the pages to follow but the second foundation for the present volume lay in that brief visit to Deering in 1949.

From 1949 to 1951 Helge Larsen was visiting professor at the University of Alaska, in Fairbanks. His collaboration with Froelich Rainey and Louis Giddings was intensified during this period and from it developed the project "the Bering Strait Expedition 1950". It was agreed that Helge Larsen should concentrate his efforts in Deering and Trail Creek, Giddings would continue his work at Cape Denbigh, while Froelich Rainey would go to Wales and work his way along the coastline towards Teller. As can be seen from the publications of the three, the collaboration was extremely productive and later on in his life Larsen often referred back to those years.

For a number of years after 1951 Larsen concentrated his efforts on fieldwork in Greenland, where he played a prominent role in the excavations that lead to the discovery of the palaeo-Eskimo Saqqaq culture (Meldgaard 1952; Larsen & Meldgaard 1958; Mathiassen 1958). During this period he also he participated in excavations in the Godthåbs fjord together with his Alaskan colleagues – Louis Giddings and Douglas Anderson, with whom he also conducted his last fieldwork in Alaska, at Cape Krusenstern in 1961.

Two years later he was appointed Head of the Ethnographic Collections at the Danish National Museum, a position he held until his retirement in 1975 when he was 70 years old. The period of Larsen's retirement forms the third point of departure for the present volume, as he now devoted himself to continuing the work on the material he collected in Alaska. Unfortunately, Larsen did not see the completion of the book before his death in 1983 but what he did leave was a substantial manuscript and virtually all of the illustrations seen in this volume.

The fourth and final point of departure for this book is based on numerous enquiries in 1997 to the Danish National Museum from people in Alaska, including inhabitants of Deering. During the laying of pipes for water a construction crew cut through new Ipiutak remains (Reanier et al. 1998; Mason 2000) and a pressing need for the publication of the volume once more arose; both as a consideration to the people of Deering and for the benefit of the scientific society in general. The enquiries from Deering lead Dr. Jørgen

Meldgaard, who participated in the excavations at both Deering and Trail Creek, to travel to Deering with the papers of immediate relevance. Upon his return the preparation of this volume was initiated.

On behalf of Helge Larsen the present editor wishes to express his gratitude to the Rask-Ørsted Fund, the Danish Expedition Fund, the Knud Rasmussen Fund, the Wenner-Gren Foundation and the Arctic Institute of North America which made the fieldwork in Deering possible. Helge Larsen would furthermore have wished to thank Dr. Hans Christian Gulløv, the artist and cultural historian Jens Rosing and photographer Lennart Larsen for their invaluable assistance in the production of the illustrations.

On my own behalf I would like to thank the Knud Rasmussen Fund, the Danish Research Council for Humanities and SILA – the Greenland Research Centre at the National Museum of Denmark for providing the means to realize the manuscript on Deering. Dr. Erle Nelson (Simon Fraser University, B.C.) and Jennifer Newton (University of Alaska, Fairbanks) made an important contribution by transforming our Danish-English it into a single language.

Helge Larsen, and his work in Alaska, figure prominently in the memories of Arctic researchers working with the Ethnographical Collections today. A substantial part of those memories can be directly attributed to the vital role played by the people of Deering and by numerous of colleagues with whom Helge Larsen held continuous discussion on the prehistory and history of Alaska. He would also have wished to extent his warm gratitude to these people.

Finally, I would like to comment on the editing of the manuscript. The intention has been to change as little of Helge Larsen's manner of speech as possible. Furthermore, the list of references and some of the illustrations were incomplete at the time of Larsen's death, therefore, any resultant errors are solely the responsibility of the editor.

Martin Appelt
The Danish National Museum, October 2001

REFERENCES

Birket-Smith, Kaj
1929: The Caribou Eskimos. Report of the Fifth Thule Expedition, vol. V. Copenhagen.

Giddings, Louis J.
1951: The Denbigh Flint Complex. American Antiquity, vol. XVI (3). Salt Lake City.

Koch, Lauge
1940-45: Survey of North Greenland – IV. Danish Expeditions to East and North Greenland (North of 79° N. lat.) Second Period 1933-38. Meddelelser om Grønland bd. 130(1). København.

Larsen, Helge
1934: Dødemandsbugten – An Eskimo Settlement on Clavering Island. Meddelelser om Grønland, bd. 102(1).

1938: Archaeological Investigations in Knud Rasmussen Land. Meddelelser om Grønland, bd. 119(8)

1950a: De dansk-amerikanske Alaska-ekspeditioner 1949-50. Geografisk Tidsskrift bd. 50. København.

1950b: Archaeological Investigations in Southwestern Alaska. American Antiquity, vol. 15(3). Salt Lake City.

1954: The position of Ipiutak in Eskimo Culture. American Antiquity, vol. 1. Salt Lake City.

1982: Eskimo and Indian Means of Transport, their Relationships and Distribution. In (ed. Hultkrantz, Åke & Ørnulf Vorren) The Hunters – their Culture and Way of Life, Tromsø Museum Skrifter, vol. XVIII. Universitetsforlaget. Tromsø – Oslo – Bergen.

Larsen, Helge & Froelich Rainey
1948: Ipiutak and the Arctic Whale Hunting Culture. Anthropological Papers of the American Museum of Natural History, vol. 42.

Larsen, Helge & Jørgen Meldgaard
1958: Paleo-Eskimo Cultures in Disko Bugt, West Greenland. Meddelelser om Grønland, bd. 161(2). Copenhagen.

Mason, Owen K.
2000: Ipiutak/Birnirk relationships in Northwest Alaska: Master and Slave or Partners in Trade? In (Ed. Appelt, Martin, Joel Berglund & Hans Christian Gulløv) Identities and Cultural Contacts in the Arctic. Danish Polar Center Publications No. 8.

Mathiassen, Therkel
1931: Ancient Eskimo Settlements in the Kangâmiut Area. Meddelelser om Grønland bd. 91(1). København.

1958: The Sermermiut Excavations 1955. Meddelelser om Grønland, bd. 161(3). Copenhagen.

Meldgaard, Jørgen
1952: A Palaeo-Eskimo Culture in West Greenland. American Antiquity, vol. 17 (3). Salt Lake City.

Reanier, Richard, Glenn W. Sheehan & Anne M. Jensen
1998: Report of 1997 field discoveries, city of Deering Safe Water Cultural Resource Project. Report to Ukpeagvik Inupiaq Corporation (UIC), Barrow.

Steensby, H.P.
1916: An anthropogeographical study of the origin of the Eskimo culture. Meddelelser om Grønland bd. 53

List of Illustrations

Fig. 1 Western part of Deering, with excavation area (photo H. Larsen)

Fig. 2 The northern part of central Seward Peninsula (drawing M. Appelt)

Fig. 3 *Tupeq* (Imnachermiut winterhouse) on the east side of the river mouth, excavated in 1950 by author (photo H. Larsen).

Fig. 4 *Qalegi* – 1st floor layer (photo H. Larsen).

Fig. 5 *Qalegi* – 1st floor layer (drawing H.C. Gulløv & M. Appelt).

Fig. 6 *Qalegi* – 1st floor layer, SW corner (photo H. Larsen)

Fig. 7 *Qalegi* – 1st floor layer, concentration of artefacts in NW corner (photo H. Larsen).

Fig. 8 *Qalegi* – 1st floor layer, stakes that may have supported a container (photo H. Larsen).

Fig. 9 *Qalegi* – 1st floor layer, hearth (photo H. Larsen).

Fig. 10 Cross section through hearth area (drawing M. Appelt).

Fig. 11 *Qalegi* – 1st floor layer, "handles" in one of the wall logs (photo H. Larsen).

Fig. 12 *Qalegi* – Shingle-layer separating the 1st and 2nd floor layers (photo H. Larsen).

Fig. 13 *Qalegi* – 3rd floor layer, seen from East (photo H. Larsen).

Fig. 14 *Qalegi* – 3rd floor layer (drawing H.C. Gulløv & M. Appelt).

Fig. 15 *Qalegi* – 3rd floor layer, seen from West (photo H. Larsen).

Fig. 16 *Qalegi* – 3rd floor layer, with portion of the 1st floor layer left en the SW corner, seen from East (photo H. Larsen).

Fig. 17 An attempt at reconstructing the *Qalegi* (drawing H.C.Gulløv).

Fig. 18 Bow with "hand guard" from White River, Yukon (photo Frederick Johnson).

Fig. 19 Harpoon heads, type 1 (a) and 2 (b) (drawing J. Rosing).

Fig. 20 Harpoon socket piece, approx. 6 cm long (drawing J. Rosing).

Fig. 21 Throwing stick with animal features, 13 cm long (drawing J. Rosing).

Fig. 22 Throwing stick with animal features, 16.2 cm long (drawing J. Rosing).

Fig. 23 (clockwise) Sled runner (P7361), snowshoe frame piece (P7357), arrowhead (P7972), snowbeater? (P7632), snowbeater? (P7372) and barbed harpoon head (P7926). Scale approx. 1:4 (photo L. Larsen).

Fig. 24 An attempt at reconstructing (by Keld Jessen Hansen) the Deering sled (drawing H.C. Gulløv).

Fig. 25 Toy sled from Ungava Bay, Labrador (photo Smithsonian Institution – Cat No. 89941).

Fig. 26 Model of build-up sled (photo L. Larsen).

Fig. 27 An attempted reconstructing of the Deering sled (drawing J. Rosing).

Fig. 28 (a) Reconstructed Deering snowshoe and (b) a King's Island snowshoe, after Davidson 1937 (drawing by H.C. Gulløv)

Fig. 29 Toy canoe-like vessel with carved figure in the middle, from the *Qalegi*. The vessel is 21.4 cm long (photo L. Larsen).

Fig. 30 Shovel blade from *Qalegi*. The blade is 41 cm long (photo L. Larsen).

Fig. 31 Grass mat from *Qalegi* – 3rd floor layer, 26 cm long (photo L. Larsen).

Fig. 32 Fire-drill and hearth from SW corner of *Qalegi* (photo L. Larsen).

Fig. 33 Ornamented flaker handles, (a) is 16.4 cm long (drawings J. Rosing).

I. Deering and the Imnachermiut

Deering, a small village with a long row of wooden houses, a school, a store and with 181 inhabitants in 1950, lies at Kotzebue Sound about 60 miles due south of Kotzebue. The village is situated in a bight flanked to the west by the white cliffs of Cape Deceit and to the east by a steep, rocky point which forms the northern end of a low, rounded mountain ridge that continues inland in a southerly direction. At the foot of this ridge flows the Imnachuck River,[1] a shallow, clear stream which rises in the mountains about 25 miles southeast of Deering. For a major part of its course it meanders slowly toward the coast, through a wide belt of willows, which in the last few miles changes to low, marshy tundra, with numerous lakes and dead river branches (Fig. 1). Just before it reaches the sea, a beach ridge running parallel to the coast forces the river to change its course to the east until it finally breaks through

the beach ridge and enters Kotzebue Sound. It is on the long, narrow strip of land between the river and the sea that Deering is situated. A number of recent house pits on the east side of the river mouth indicate former habitation, but only one family remained in 1950.

Location on a beach ridge, often near the outlet of river, is a feature Deering shares with most coastal villages in western and northern Alaska, recent as well as prehistoric. This is simply due to the fact that for hundreds of miles the coast consists of tundra-covered silt deposits and the only places suitable for habitation are where sea currents and wave action have formed well drained gravel beach ridges. In contrast to places like Point Hope, Cape Krusenstern, Point Spencer, and Platinum that consist of a number of parallel beach ridges separated by swales, at Deering there is only one beach ridge, though very wide. The

Fig. 1: Western part of Deering, with excavation area (photo H. Larsen).

[1] The native name of the river; on local maps it is called Inmachuk.

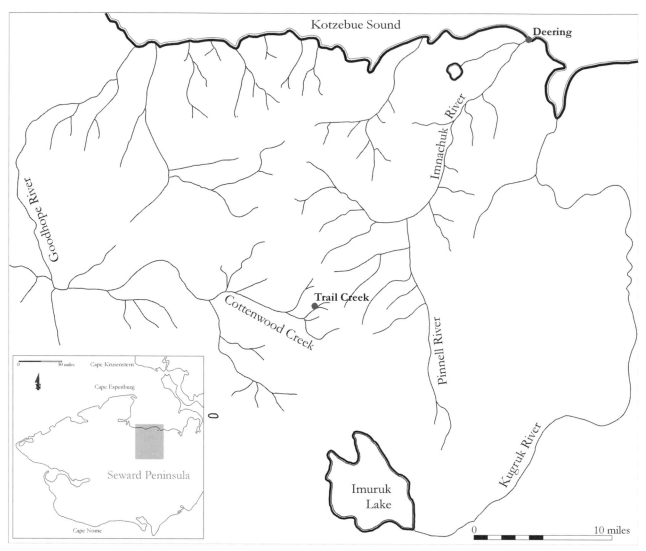

Fig. 2: The northern part of central Seward Peninsula (drawing M. Appelt).

reason for this is probably that Deering is situated at the head of the rather shallow Kotzebue Sound while the other four sites are exposed to the open sea. To the archaeologist, this means that Deering does not offer the possibility for beach ridge dating.[2] All habitation, both present and former, is concentrated on the one ridge. As we shall see presently it has been occupied, at least sporadically, for more than a thousand years.

Like several other towns and villages in Alaska, the present village owes its existence to the gold-rush at the turn of the century; probably the greatest event in Alaska's history and the one that ultimately led to statehood. When the tens of

thousands of stampeders arrived in Nome in the summer of 1900 and discovered that the beach at Nome was neither as large nor as rich in gold as they had been told, the majority decided to return to the States or try their fortune in other parts of the territory. Some remained however, and began to investigate the possibilities of Seward Peninsula. In a remarkably short time there was hardly a creek that had not been scouted by prospectors, and mining camps sprang up like mushrooms all over the peninsula. Imnachuck and creeks that proved to be gold-bearing were no exceptions, and only a year after the Nome stampede, horse-drawn wagons loaded with goods for the mining camps on the north side of Seward Peninsula were bumping along over a hastily formed trail

[2] Giddings 1967: 16.

between Nome and Kotzebue Sound. The trail followed Imnachuck to the coast, and it was here, at the end of the trail, that Deering grew up.

At first there was only a roadhouse and a store, but already in 1902 the government built a school for the Eskimos who had been attracted by the store and the white man with all his desirable goods. It seems, however, that the Eskimos were cautious and did not want to be too close to the white men, and they, or at least some of them, built their houses on the east side of the river, while the white establishments were on the other side. This we learnt from one of the natives of Deering, John Douglas, who among other things told us that a house ruin we excavated on the east side of the river was inhabited in 1902. Judging from their state of preservation, the other house pits there seem to be of a similar age. The excavation showed us that the natives in 1902 still lived in their original form of dwelling, which will be described later. We do not know when they gave them up in favor of the wooden houses or shacks they live in today.

John Douglas furnished us with another bit of interesting information; namely that he and his family were the only people now living in Deering who had lived there before 1900. In other words, they alone could call themselves and did consider themselves Imnachermiut, i.e. the people that live at Imnachuck. This is confirmed by the census of 1950 from which it appears that, apart from the children and the younger people of whom the majority were born in Deering, the population of Deering is made up of people who have come from 20 different localities. Shishmaref, halfway between Kotzebue and Wales, has been the source of the largest contingent, next are villages on the Kobuk River, then Tapqaq (Cape Espenberg) at the entrance to Kotzebue Sound and Kotzebue. Some have also come from places as remote as Point Hope, Kivalina, Wales, and Cape Nome. Even the Imnachermiut presumably did not live at Deering proper, or at least not permanently. John Douglas' sister, Mary Morris (Ajaitiak), who was born at Kobuk Lake in 1879, said that her family used to spend the winter at a camp two miles upriver from Deering. Her

brother John added that when his father was a child, Deering was a trading place like Kotzebue, though no people lived there permanently. Finally Qoperluk, the oldest man in Deering who was born about 1870 in a camp on the Kugruk River, the next river east of Imnachuck, remembered that he, when he was about 6 years old, stayed at Deering one spring where his family was hunting seal. He did not mention what the family did in the summer, but in the fall they packed all their belongings on dogs and went inland. They usually spent the winter on a river he called Fish River, where they trapped fox and hunted caribou.

At the present time there are no caribou on Seward Peninsula and they have not been sighted for half a century. According to John Douglas, caribou became scarce around 1900 and from the accounts of Qoperluk and Ajaitjak we can assume that caribou must have been plentiful in the first part of the 1800s and probably even until the middle of that century. "Before my father was married there was lots of caribou here" said Qoperluk. His father hunted them with bow and arrow or speared them from his kayak. Their favourite hunting method however seems to have been the caribou drive or *kangeraq*, a circular enclosure into which the caribou were driven between mile-long rows of *inuksut*, willows tied together in bundles that looked like men standing up. Ajaitjak relates that her grandmother as a young girl used to run after the caribou and chase them toward the *kangeraq*. "Caribou were plentiful at that time", she said. The use of the *kangeraq* is well known from northern-most Alaska[3] but while the enclosures there consisted of snares placed in concentric circles, the Imnachermiut used a fence of willows. When the caribou came inside the fence the hunters who had been hiding outside the fence shot them. The *kangeraq* used by Ajaitiak's father was very large and situated between Imnachuck and Old Glory Creek, not far from Trail Creek, and it is not unlikely that the occupants of the Trail Creek caves used the same location for hunting caribou.[4] Another *kangeraq* used by the Imnachermiut was on the other side of Sullivan Creek (the stream just west of Imnachuck), on a knoll called *Kangeraruraq*. Here the fence was made of driftwood. Further west the Tapqaq people used a *kangeraq* on Devil Mountain, south of

[3] Ipiutak:: 34; Larsen 1958a: 576.
[4] Larsen 1968.

Tapqaq. In the summertime they hunted caribou from kayaks in a lake east of Devil Mountain. Like the Nunamuit of northern Alaska the Imnachermiut also used to catch caribou in snares set in willow thickets. Ajaitiak's father usually had his snares at a place called Pitaruk (now Horseshoe Bend) on the Inmachuck, 11 miles from Deering. Incidentally, caribou were hunted all the year round, and as Ajaitiak said: "It was the only food (probably meaning staple food) we had, except in the spring when we went to Tapqaq to hunt seal".

There can hardly be any doubt that caribou were the main source of food for the Imnachermiut until it disappeared around the turn of the century. Next in importance were seals, particularly the ringed seal, but also the large *ugruk* or bearded seal. The best hunting season for both species was the spring, when the seals crawl up upon the ice to lie in the sun, but they were also caught with net in the fall, and under the ice in winter. In this connection it is interesting to notice that the Douglas family, as the only family in Deering, maintained the right to a certain nearby netting place which they claimed was the property of their family, and reluctantly the other villagers respected this hereditary right.

According to Ajaitiak, spring sealing took place from the end of April and continued until the ice broke up in July. When the time came to begin sealing they put their *umiak* and all their belongings on a sled, which they and the dogs pulled out to Tapqaq. They must have had very few dogs compared to the Alaskan Eskimo of today, as Ajaitiak said that at that time, five dogs were many. At Tapqaq they lived out on the ice until it became too rotten , then they moved to the beach where they stayed for the rest of the sealing season. On the ice they lived in a domeshaped tent, *itjernik*, which like the *itjerlik* of the Nunamuit[5] consisted of a framework of willow branches covered with a layer of caribou, *ugruk* or seal skin. It was furnished with a window of *ugruk*- intestine and had a skin door. A tipi-like tent, the *napakshak*, was also used on the beach. This was the same as the *napaqtak* of the Nunamuit[6]. The seals were stalked and the hunter had to be very clever in order to sneak close enough to hit the prey with a

harpoon. Kayaks were used whenever there was open water.

When all the ice was gone the Imnachermiut returned to the river, where some hunted ground squirrel, others hunted caribou, while still others went fishing. In the month of August, when the salmon run is at its peak, we must assume that the Imnachermiut came together at the mouth of Imnachuck to catch their share of this valuable fish. We only know that they fished salmon in August, either spearing or catching them in fish weirs made of willow. Judging from the numerous and large shoals of salmon, which in 1950 came close to the village shore in 1950 and by the thousands tried to ascend the river, salmon fishing, at least in good years, must have played a very important role in the economy of the Imnachermiut.

To complete the list of food resources that were available to the Imnachermiut, we should mention that birds of various kinds were hunted with bird spear, bow and arrow and bolas, or were snared. As well, women gathered a great variety of berries, leaves and roots which were stored in whole seal carcasses with or without the blubber. Before we close the subject of food, it should be mentioned that the Imnachermiut never hunted large baleen whales. This is a significant cultural difference between the Imnachermiut and the Eskimos at Wales.

According to Ajaitiak, the Imnachermiut spent the winter at a place two miles south of Deering, and she mentioned explicitly that this village was only occupied in wintertime. When she and Qoperluk talked about winterhouses they both used the term *tupeq*, which is surprising considering that *tupeq* among other Eskimo means tent. We find the word again in another form, *tupeqeruk*, which is the Imnachermiut name for a temporary dwelling built on top of the ground and consisting of a framework of willow branches covered with moss turf (*iwrut*). A hut of this type was seen by the author in 1942 still standing near the Utorqaq River and was called a *iwrulik* by the Utorqarmiut. In contrast to this temporary dwelling the *tupeq* of the Imnachermiut was dug down into the ground. The walls were made of upright timbers and the wall and roof were covered with *iwrut* and a layer of dirt. It had a short entrance passage, the bottom of which was below floor level with an *ugruk* skin

[5] Larsen 1958: 575-76.
[6] Larsen 1958: 577.

Fig. 3: Tupeq *(Imnachermiut winterhouse) on the east side of the river mouth, excavated in 1950 by author (photo H. Larsen).*

as an outside door. There was no door between the entrance passage and the room. According to Ajaitiak, within the room there were sleeping places around a central fireplace lined with stones. The sleeping places were covered with willows, on which "rich people" laid caribou skins. Directly above the fireplace was an opening which, when the fire was burning low or out, was closed with a window made *ugruk* intestine.

A house of this type situated on the east side of the river mouth was excavated in 1950 and illustrates many of the traits mentioned by our informants. It was oblong in outline, with its greatest extension (5,50 m) at right angles to the entrance passage, which was 3.50 m long and 0.80 m wide; from front to the rear wall it measured 4.25 m. As seen in fig. 3, the central part of the room had a wooden flooring of hewn planks surrounding an almost square fireplace lined with flat stones standing on edge. The floor slanted slightly toward the entrance passage, the bottom of which was 0.40 m below the first board. The inner part of the entrance passage was supported by upright poles, the outer part by a 1.50 m long horizontal log on each side. Parts of the walls of the house were preserved (see fig. 3). They consisted of upright poles stuck down into the sand, most 5

cm thick and some 70 cm long. In the walls were six heavier posts, four in the corners, which undoubtedly would have supported the roof. The sleeping places, one on each side of the floor, consisted of pure sand; on the right were two planks and near the wall, two drying racks (*paneqsetit*) consisting of a number of thin, round sticks that fitted into holes in two straight side pieces. At the middle of the rear wall was a 1.25 m deep and 1.50 m wide recess, which probably had been used for storage. Standing in the middle of the floor was a round wooden bowl containing a strange mixture of Eskimo tools such as whetstones, knife and *ulo* blades of slate, several iron objects, a powder flask, and a revolver. The house is almost identical to houses excavated by the author in 1942 at Aqergognat and Icy Cape, south of Wainwright.[7] The Utorqarmiut called this type of house *akilgere*, a name that was also familiar to John Douglas. Very similar to this type are the houses excavated by J. L. Giddings at the Ambler Island site on the Kobuk River[8].

The Imnachermiut also used snow houses, but only when traveling. The *aniguijak*[9] was built of blocks of snow and partly dug down into a drift of hard snow. It was round and had vertical walls on top of which were stuck willows that were bent and tied together. Small willows were used to fill out the space between the rafters and then snow was piled top with a snow shovel (*poilerin*). There was no hallway but snow blocks were put up in

---

[7] Ipiutak: fig. 9.
[8] Giddings 1952: fig. 8.
[9] The same name was used the Nunamiut for snowhouses built of snow blocks.

front as a windbreaker and a caribou or seal skin was used as a door. Qoperluk said that a semi lunar stone lamp was used in the snow house, but according to Ajaitiak, snow houses were un-heated. Most likely a lamp was used, at least for illumination, though cooking was done outside. For this, a fire was built in a hole dug down to the ground and in this stones were heated until they became red hot. These were dumped into a wooden dish filled with water and food until it was cooked.

The various culture traits mentioned above should suffice to give an impression of the life of the Imnachermiut before the prospectors and traders appeared on the scene. This chapter was meant to serve a double purpose; firstly as background for the following description of the main excavation at Deering, by describing the food resources of the area and how an Eskimo population made use of them and adapted themselves to the natural conditions of this particular place. Secondly, the purpose was to demonstrate the great similarity in modes of life between the Imnachermiut and the Nunamiut of northernmost Alaska. The two groups have so many and such significant traits in common that I feel they belong to the same or very similar variants of the Eskimo culture. The following description indicates that this similarity has its roots in an old, common tradition.

II. The Excavation of a House Belonging to the Ipiutak Culture

Flying over Deering in the summer, one is struck by the sharp contrast between the drab colors of the surrounding landscape and the lush green of the outer, inhabited part of the beach ridge that separates the lower reaches of Imnachuck from the sea. The luxuriant vegetation around the houses is of course due to a soil rich in organic material and nutritive salts, a sure sign of long occupation. This was confirmed by the occurrence of cultural remains in every test pit we dug between the houses. However, it was not by test digging, but purely by accident, that Deering was discovered as an exceptionally interesting archaeological site. During an unintentional stopover on our way to Trail Creek in 1949,[10] Charles Lucier and I noticed two dark layers containing animal bones and some artifacts in a bank at the seashore west of the village, where there is a landing field for aeroplanes. A brief investigation showed that the uppermost layers, separated from the lower by sterile gravel, represented modern or recent-prehistoric Eskimo culture, while arrowheads and pottery sherds decorated with concentric circles clearly showed that the lower layer belonged to the Western Thule culture phase.[11] We did not get very far with our investigation before an Eskimo boy who had been watching us called our attentions to a place on the riverside of the landing field where he had found "old stuff". That we immediately abandoned our newly discovered "site" is understandable considering that his "old stuff" consisted exclusively of specimens belonging to the Ipiutak culture.

The site where he had made his finds is situated on the beach ridge where the river changes its course from a northerly to an easterly direction. Here, virtually on the riverbank, was a patch of very tall grass where the children had been playing and found artifacts. The holes they had dug revealed that only a thin layer of gravel covered a dark and loose, almost powdery, soil with numerous wooden chips, willow sticks, and remains of

dry grass. Out of the gravel protruded the surface of two long, heavy, horizontal logs at right angles to each other, and when the grass was cleared away two more logs appeared which with the other two formed an almost square frame of about 9 x 9 m. We soon realized that the frame was the walls of an unusually large house, and at the time we had not yet found all of it. That it belonged to the Ipiutak culture was obvious from the specimens we had already seen and of which we soon found more. What surprised us and for a while kept us in doubt about the antiquity of the find, was the incredibly good state of preservation of the logs, the wooden objects, the willow twigs and the grass we found in the dark soil in the house. It was not frozen, so why was it all so well preserved so close to the surface? I received an explanation some years later from Mr. John Cross, one of Alaska's oldest bush pilots.

According to John Cross the landing field at Deering – the first on Seward Peninsula – was made in 1922 by the famous Norwegian arctic explorer Roald Amundsen, who intended to use it in connection with a planned polar flight. In order to make the landing field (which by the way was never used for its original purpose) they had to fill in several house pits situated between the Ipiutak house and the sea. In 1945, John Cross had the field enlarged so that it could be used for commercial traffic. As part of this operation he had to remove a mound that was situated exactly where we found the Ipiutak house. The mound, which was approximately 40 feet long, 30 feet wide and 8 feet high, was covered with grass and consisted of dark, loose earth. On the south side were some burials, primarily of children, and a Deering family had a cold storage on the north side. No logs or other wood parts of a house were encountered until they hit the logs we found and which at that time were covered by one foot of frozen soil. This was the explanation for the good preservation. The logs and what was inside the house had been permanently frozen until the mound was removed, and four summers' thawing had not been enough to start decomposition. We were

---

[10] Larsen 1968.
[11] Ipiutak: 170 and Pl. 95.

Fig. 4: Qalegi – *1ˢᵗ floor layer (photo H. Larsen).*

thus extremely lucky, in the first place because John Cross and his crew had reached the level of the field and did not have to go deeper, and secondly, that the house had been exposed long enough to thaw it out so that we could go right ahead with our excavation without being hampered by frost.

In 1949 the investigation was limited to the digging of a test pit, but in June 1950 we returned with a team consisting of students from the University of Alaska and the Danish National Museum and completed the excavation of the house and of two adjoining areas, in all 220 m². Because of the special character of the site the excavation will be described as it proceeded.

Having removed the layer of gravel that had covered the house since the bulldozer had been at work, we exposed a floor consisting of very fine, black dirt mixed with, and in places completely covered by, chips and splinters of wood, more or less worked pieces of wood, willow sticks, and grass (fig. 4). In some places, for instance along the south wall where there had been a low platform or bench, there was a regular layer of grass that was obviously cut and carried into the house to be used as a platform-cover. The top layer was of uneven thickness; greatest in the outer part of the room, but toward the center it was paper-thin in many places. As it was resting on gravel, it was often difficult to discern.

As may be seen on the ground-plan (fig. 5) and on fig. 6, in the southwestern corner there were a number of flat, hewn boards and round logs, more or less parallel with the south wall, which probably formed part of a platform. The longest piece is a round log that was held in place by two stakes: one on each side. Similar stakes may be seen on

either side of the 3.20 m long log that was lying parallel to the west wall and probably served as the edge of a 1.40 m wide platform. A double row of stakes holding a short log in place is also seen in the northwest corner. There a number of artifacts, among them the side of a box, a firedrill, and a paddle shaped wooden object, were lying on the floor (fig. 7). Two short poles extending from the west and east wall and parallel with the north wall are probably parts of the edge of a third platform. It thus seems as though there were platforms or benches along three of the walls, while there are no signs of a platform along the east wall. As we shall see later, we presume that the entrance was here.

Parallel to the walls and in front of the platforms was a row of post holes, sometimes two or three close together, but most of them evenly spaced and together forming a square around the central fireplace. Though a few are missing, there can be no doubt that there were twelve posts and that their function was to support the roof. The double and triple holes probably mean that either two or three posts were used together or more likely that some of the posts have been moved. Several of the posts have been supported by wooden stakes or pegs, which in some cases we found in place along the edge of the hole. Seven short stakes forming a circle about 40 cm in diameter were found at the edge of the northern platform, but had no connection with a post hole and might have been used to support a container or bowl of skin, possibly for cooking with hot stones (fig. 8).

In the center of the house was an almost square fireplace, 2.20 x 1.80 m, with ashes in the middle and short wooden stakes along the edge (fig. 9). The stakes are placed similarly to an earlier fireplace, (fig. 10) and supported thin logs that formed a frame around the fireplace.

On the second day of the excavation we discovered that the logs forming the north and south walls continued about 3.5 m beyond the east wall where they were connected by logs forming a new termination of the house to the east. We now had an oblong house instead of a square one, with two

Fig. 5: Qalegi – *1ˢᵗ floor layer (drawing H.C. Gulløv & M. Appelt)*.

rooms; a large, almost square main room and a smaller, rectangular anteroom, as we call it for reasons to be discussed later. The house was now about 12 m long and 8 m wide in the middle. Due

mainly to the position of 11.70 m long log that formed the south wall, the ground plan was trapezoidal rather than rectangular. Off hand, one would be inclined to believe that the ground plan

Fig. 6: Qalegi – *1ˢᵗ floor layer, SW corner (photo H. Larsen)*.

Fig. 7: Qalegi – *1ˢᵗ floor layer, concentration of artefacts in NW corner (photo H. Larsen)*.

Fig. 8: Qalegi – 1st *floor layer, stakes that may have supported a container (photo H. Larsen).*

Fig. 9: Qalegi – 1st *floor layer, hearth (photo H. Larsen).*

originally formed a rectangle and that the apparent irregularity is due to later displacement of the logs, particularly of the south wall, but this is contradicted by the fact that the rows of postholes and the logs that formed the platform edges are parallel to the walls as we found them. Actually the house was 8.20 m wide in the west end and 7 m wide in the east end (both inside measurements). Measured across the fireplace the main room was 7.60 m from east to west and 8.0 m in the opposite direction. The dimensions of the anteroom were 7.20 x 3.20 m.

The walls were made of heavy, straight tree trunks that had been trimmed of branches but otherwise not worked, except for the strange "handles" in some of the logs (fig. 11), which will be described later. The walls consisted of two logs on top of each other (the top log in the east wall had fallen down), and if there originally were more they must have been removed a long time ago, because according to John Cross no heavy logs were found when they bulldozed the place. The dimensions of the logs, of which the longest was 40 cm in diameter, raises questions about their place of origin as well as transportation. The logs were of spruce and today the nearest spruce forest with trees of such dimensions is at the Kobuk, and it is not very likely that they could be found closer at the time of the Ipiutak culture. Though we must not exclude the possibility that the trees were cut on the Kobuk, it is more reasonable to assume that they are driftwood; even so they must have been transported over a considerable distance. To our knowledge, no rivers carry-

ing such heavy timber empty into Kotzebue Sound, so it seems that the logs must have been transported either on sleds, or more likely towed by boats from some ocean shore. Wherever they originated, their transportation must have been quite an achievement and called for the collaboration of many people. That is one of the reasons why at an early stage of the excavation we came to the conclusion that the house was not an ordinary dwelling, but a communal house of some sort; probably a men's house. We shall return to this point later and continue the description of the excavation of the main room after the floor had been exposed.

Under the floor was a 5-15 cm thick layer of gravel or rather shingle of nut-sized and larger stones and flat beach pebbles (fig. 12). At first we thought that this was the result of a transgression of the sea, but when we discovered that this layer did not occur in either the anteroom nor in sections we excavated outside the house there remained only one explanation, namely that the gravel was carried into the house and spread over the floor of the main room. The reason for this is either that the floor had become too muddy, or that the gravel was laid during the reopening of the house after a period in which it was not used. As we shall see later, it was not the only time that this form of "house cleaning" had taken place. The posts have remained standing because the postholes with the supporting stakes protrude through a gravel layer and down into what appeared to be a second floor. The fireplace had the same shape and size, and the same round

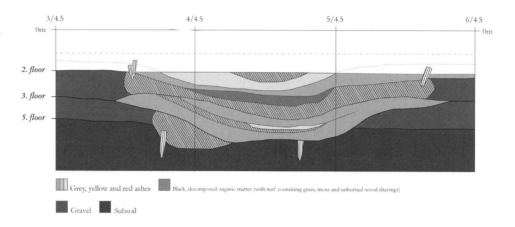

Fig. 10: Cross section through hearth area (drawing M. Appelt).

3/4.5   4/4.5   5/4.5   6/4.5

2. floor
3. floor
5. floor

▦ Grey, yellow and red ashes   ▦ Black, decomposed organic matter (with turf containing grass, moss and unburned wood shavings)

■ Gravel   ■ Subsoil

patch of yellow ashes in the center, as on the floor above. There were no logs at the platform edges; they might have been removed before the gravel was put on and possibly used again.

Evidence of a period in which the house was abandoned for some time was found under floor number two. Separating this from an earlier floor (no. 3) was a 15-20 cm thick layer of organic material; mostly sod blocks, but also containing black, loose dirt with plant remains. This layer covered the entire room, including the fireplace. The fact that there was not a continuous layer of sod, but rather blocks lying in the loose dirt, seems to indicate that these were originally part of the roof and/or the walls, and that the house had collapsed. There were no sods in the black material that covered the fireplace, which may indicate that there was a smoke hole directly above it. It seems that at least most of the posts remained standing through subsequent rebuilding, because

the holes – and in some cases the base of the posts themselves – were found in both floor number three and in the same places as in the later floors.

The third floor was very well defined (fig. 13) with a mass of wood chips around the fireplace and a layer of grass and plaited grass-mats (fig. 14) on the platforms, the surface of which was 6-10 cm lower than the floor. Parallel to the south wall, a 3 m long log formed the edge of the south platform. In addition to the twelve postholes mentioned above, there was an extra post in the northern row and two holes close together at the northeastern corner. The fireplace was almost square, with a circular depression – 1.8 m in diameter – surrounded by a frame consisting of four thin poles held in place by short stakes, mainly in the corners. Patches of gray ashes were found in two places near the east wall and in the northwest corner.

Underneath the third floor was another layer of

Fig. 11: Qalegi – 1st floor layer, "handles" in one of the wall logs (photo H. Larsen).

Fig. 12: Qalegi – Shingle-layer separating the 1st and 2nd floor layers (photo H. Larsen).

sterile gravel or shingle, about 5 cm thick and obviously brought in and spread over another underlying floor. This, the fourth floor, was not as conspicuous as the floor above, but was composed of a distinct thin, black layer below the gravel and on top of another layer of gravel that can only be interpreted as a result of occupation, although of short duration, probably only one season.

Under a 10-20 cm thick layer of gravel was another floor, the fifth and last. Actually, it was the first floor of the house . It was well defined, consisting of black dirt with wood chips and, particularly on the platforms, grass. The postholes from the floors above were also in this floor, in addition to others (indicated with dotted lines on the ground plan of the 3rd. floor). There was only one horizontal log on the floor, a one meter long piece at the edge of the south platform.

The fireplace, a small heap of gravel with ashes on top, was surrounded by a shallow, 50 cm wide, horseshoe-shaped ditch. At one end of this there was a circular, 30 cm wide, deep hole, half of which was lined with vertical wooden stakes and narrow planks that were burnt on the inside and contained yellow ashes. No explanation for the purpose of this hole may be offered.

The floor-layer rested on sterile gravel, which at the time the house was built must have formed the surface, because in places there were patches of partly withered, short grass on the root (The

same kind of grass-covered surface was found under the refuse in Field A and B excavated respectively west and east of the house). In other words, the house had been built on top of the ground!

THE ANTEROOM

The excavation of the eastern end of the house, as seen on the ground plan (fig. 5 and fig. 14), was separated from the rest by heavy logs, revealing that it had not served the same purpose as the main room. We did not find floor layers, separated by layers of gravel, corresponding to those in the main room. In fact, apart from some gravel midway in front of the main separating log – where there obviously had been an opening – there was no gravel in the room other than at the bottom. The gravel layers of the main room ended sharply at the logs separating the main room from the anteroom and the little gravel there was in the anteroom was undoubtedly the result of people passing through the opening between the two rooms. That there had been an opening here is also evident from the presence of a 50 cm wide, deep cut in the separating log. Furthermore, the only place in the anteroom where there were horizontal layers – reminiscent of the floors in the main room – was in the area between this opening and the middle of the east of the house, where the

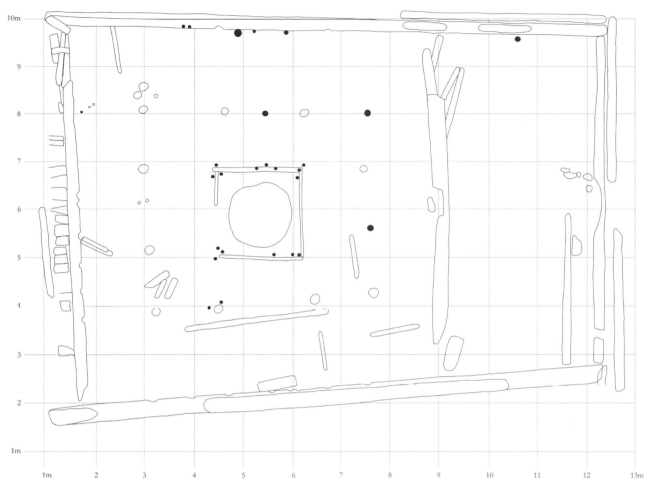

Fig. 14: Qalegi – 3*rd* *floor layer (drawing H.C. Gulløv & M. Appelt).*

Fig. 15: Qalegi – 3*rd* *floor layer, seen from West.*

main log was worn as if people had stepped on it. In other words, there were strong indications of the main entrance to the house being in the middle of the east wall, and that people walked through the anteroom in order to get into the main room. It is also possible that the three postholes in the anteroom near the inner entrance and another near the outer entrance may have served some purpose in connection with the entrances.

The debris that filled the anteroom was different from that of the main room. It consisted of many layers of loose dirt filled with wood shavings and chips, willow sticks, many animal bones, and dog faeces separated by layers of thin slabs of moss-turf, of which some were lying horizontal but many were at an angle. This turf probably came from the walls and/or roof, the layers in between had a midden-like character. In this connection it should be mentioned that there were relatively few animal bones in the main room. It seemed as though the anteroom had not been used as a living quarters, although the abundance of wood shavings and chips indicate that it may have been used as a workshop. It should be pointed out however, that debris very similar to that found in the anteroom occurred outside the east wall. From the abundance of dog faeces and hair in the anteroom it is evident that the dogs had access to the room.

FIELD A

An area of 56 m² was excavated just outside the west wall of the house. The surface of this area (Field A) consisted of the same loose gravel which covered the rest of the landing field. Below it was a dense sod that probably constituted the surface before the leveling of the landing field, underneath this were alternating layers of flat sod-blocks and loose dirt with wood chips to a depth of about 50-70 cm. The bottom layer consisted of an unbroken and very dark grass turf with straw and roots, resting on sterile gravel. In this layer, which was the surface when the house was built, there were at least six postholes and the remains of one post. The postholes did not form a recognizable pattern, but might have been for racks for storing or drying. Within the excavated area there were also ten round patches with ashes, undoubt-

edly fireplaces. In one of these there were fire-cracked stones, which were probably used for cooking.

As shown on the ground plan (fig. 14) there was a row of short, heavy poles or planks leaning against the wall. At this place there was also the remains of a sod wall, approximately one meter wide, consisting of horizontal layers of sod-blocks without wood chips or artifacts between them. From the sod wall the layers with sod-blocks and wood chips, mentioned above, were slanting away from the house.

FIELD B

An area of the same size as Field A, namely 56 m², was excavated outside the east end of the house. The conditions encountered in Field B were to some extent the same as in Field A. The following successive layers were evident: surface gravel, sod, alternating layers of sod-blocks and wood chips, and the old grass turf surface with remains of straw and roots. The bottom layer, which at the north side of the field was 60 cm below and at the south side was 80 cm below the present surface, rested on sterile gravel or in places on gray clay. Within the area were four fireplaces and one posthole.

The fill, particularly in front and to the north of the "entrance," differed from that of Field A, in being more loose and containing fewer sod-blocks. But the fill also contained an enormous amount of wood chips and shavings, grass, willow sticks, worked and unworked pieces of birch bark, in addition to bones and artifacts. In fact, it had the character of a regular midden. This midden-like material continued under the logs of the anteroom, indicating that the midden was there when the house was built. Only the logs of the anteroom rested on this midden, while the logs of the main room were lying directly on the old gravel or grass-covered surface.

SUMMARY AND INTERPRETATION

Having described the excavation of the house we may now summarize our observations and to the extent possible try to form an opinion of its construction and use. It was obvious from the finds that the people that built and occupied it were bearers of the Ipiutak culture. Even apart from the finds and even if the house in certain respects deviates from Ipiutak houses excavated in other parts of Alaska, it possesses enough characteristic features to support its Ipiutak origin. If we for a moment disregard the anteroom, which is unique and the function of which is uncertain, we find that the Deering house and the typical Ipiutak house at Point Hope have the following features in common: the shape and the layout of the ground plan with low sleeping platforms along three of the walls and probably an entrance in the middle of the fourth wall, a central floor space with a fireplace in the middle, and roof-supporting posts placed at the inner edge of the platforms. Since the excavation of the Deering house, 20 Ipiutak houses have been excavated at Cape Krusenstern by Douglas Anderson and others and of these 20, six (classified as type 1), correspond in many details to the Deering house. The main difference between them is that while the Deering house rested on an old surface, the Cape Krusenstern houses in question were dug in to about a meter below the sod.[12]

Of the points in which our house deviates from other Ipiutak houses, we were first struck by its size. The total length of the house was 12 m and the width 9 m, which means that the whole structure covered an area of 108 m². Even if we do not consider the anteroom as part of the house proper, we still have a room of about 64 m² or space enough for four average Point Hope Ipiutak houses. For comparison the largest house at Point Hope, House 31, was 7 x 6 m and at Cape Krusenstern House 17 was 7.5 x 6 m and House 30, 7 x 6.5 m. The unique feature of 12 roof-supporting posts, as compared to the normal four, is connected to the size of the house inasmuch as it would have taken four huge posts to support the superstructure that was necessary to cover a house of this size, not to mention the dimension of the beams that formed the frame on top of the posts. By filling in the space between the posts at the corners with two additional posts, the builders

could use timber that was easier to handle and probably also easier to find. Each row of posts was parallel to a wall and marked off the edge of one of the three platforms, of which the two side platforms (along the north and south wall) were 1.80 m wide, and the rear (west) platform was 1.40 m wide. There was no platform in the east end of the room. The platforms were lower than or level with the floor, they were covered with loose grass and loosely twined grass mats and retaining logs separated them from the floor. Unwoven grass as platform cover is also known from Cape Krusenstern.[13]

The large fireplace in the middle of the floor is also a natural consequence of the size of the room, as a larger fire was needed to heat it. While the average size of the fireplaces in the Ipiutak houses at Point Hope were 75 cm in diameter, the heap of red, yellow and gray ashes in the Deering house had a diameter of 130 cm and the almost square hearth area covered 3.6 m². In the third floor, it was framed by four rather thin poles held in place by short stakes. In the first floor, only the stakes remained to indicate the extension of the hearth area. This unusual feature in Ipiutak houses occurs also in House 40 at Cape Krusenstern[14] and is reminiscent of an arrangement in House 51 at Point Hope, which had an oblong pile of ashes in the middle of an almost rectangular area with gravel framed on three sides by rather heavy logs that separated it from the wooden floor.[15]

One of the striking features of the Deering house is the heavy timber that formed the base of the walls. In most places the walls consist of two horizontal logs on top of each other, in others two or more logs lay side by side and have obviously fallen down. The presence of a log more than 4 m long just outside the north wall as well as three logs side by side in the northeast corner, indicated the possibility that originally the walls had a third layer of logs. Considering that the logs are round and the fact that the house was built on top of the ground, one may wonder how the logs were kept in place. We may find an explanation in the presence of stakes and poles on the inside of the walls and wedges between the logs, as seen in the north wall, as well as an outer support of sod-blocks and sloping poles or planks along the west wall (fig.15).

The "handles" that occur in three of the walls

[12] Giddings and Anderson 1986.
[13] Giddings and Anderson 1986: 126.
[14] Giddings and Anderson 1986: 136.
[15] Ipiutak: fig. 8.

were the subject of much discussion among the excavators as well as the local Eskimos who followed the excavation with deep interest and frequently commented on our finds. The "handles", of which there were eight in the lower log in the south wall, four in the upper and two in the lower log in the west wall, and two in the lower log of the north wall, are bowl-shaped hollows cut into the logs in such a way that a crossbar is left in the middle (fig. 11). They are identical in shape with the "ice-anchor" Greenlanders make when they want to tie up their dog team on the ice. All agreed that something must have been tied to their "handles". Some had a broken or worn through crossbar, but nobody could give a satisfactory answer to the question of what was tied to them. Of the many suggestions I believe three deserve mentioning: 1) they were used for attaching ropes with which the logs were towed in the water or dragged over land to the site. Countering this, one could raise the objection that the "handles" occur only in some of the logs, albeit the heaviest, 2) for ropes holding the superstructure or parts of it, or 3) for ceremonial purposes. Though I personally was, and to some extend remain in favor of the second suggestion, we may not exclude the third. The local Eskimos, who believed that the house was an old *qalegi*, told us that during certain ceremonies in the *qalegi*, women were tied to the walls which could explain the presence of the "handles" Whether or not women were tied to the "handles", it is worth noticing that they only occur on the three sides where there were platforms.

While superimposed floors of flagstones or wooden planks are not unusual in Eskimo house-ruins, the practice of spreading course gravel on the floor has to my knowledge not been recorded before. Many of the Ipiutak houses at Point Hope had a gravel floor, but none of them had more than one floor layer and in many cases a very thin one indicating that the house had been occupied a short time, possibly one season. In the Deering house we distinguished five floor layers, consisting of fine, black dirt with many fragments of wood, willow sticks, and grass and in three cases separated by layers of coarse gravel or shingle. Beginning at the bottom, a 10-20 cm thick layer of relatively clean gravel covered the entire first floor level, with exception of the hearth area. A layer,

interpreted as the result of an occupation of short duration, separated it from a 5 cm thick layer of the same kind of gravel covering the whole room except for the fireplace. The third layer of gravel, separating the two uppermost floors, was 5-15 cm thick; being thickest on the platforms. The fact that the material for these three layers did not occur in the immediate proximity of the house but had to be transported (in considerable quantities) over a distance, probably from the beach, indicates the collaboration of several persons. This, as well as the transportation of the timber for the house, is indication of the house being different from the ordinary. If it actually was a *qalegi*, as already intimated, the spreading of the clean gravel might be part of the preparations for opening a season. This must have taken place at a time when there was no snow on the ground, possibly in the fall.

The hearth area was never covered by gravel, but a layer of loose, black dirt was lying on top of the hearth of the third floor, while the debris that covered the rest of the room at this level mostly consisted of sod blocks and plant remains. Apparently the house had collapsed and had been abandoned for some time. With this layer, which had a thickness of 15-20 cm, plus the three gravel layers and the actual floor layers, the amount of debris that had accumulated within the log walls reached an average thickness of no less than 80 cm, actually forming a stratified midden. The deepest part was the bottom of the fireplace, which was slightly excavated, being 93 cm below the top of the south wall. In relation to this 0-point, the average depths of the five floors were as follows: 1st. floor, 22.5 cm; 2nd floor, 37 cm; 3rd. floor, 51.5 cm; 4th floor, 56.5 cm; 5th floor, 78 cm.

As a consequence of the gradual rising of the floor level, the function of the horizontal logs as walls diminished accordingly, until the end of the occupation when they merely served as a base for the actual walls. No timbers (that could be identified as parts of walls) were found inside the house, but it is reasonable to assume that the central construction consisted of the 12 posts, presumably connected above with beams forming a square frame, which served as a support not only for the roof but also the walls. In that case, the walls must have consisted of upright, slanting timbers with their upper ends resting against this

Fig. 16: Qalegi – 3rd floor layer, with portion of the 1st floor layer left en the SW corner, seen from East (photo H. Larsen).

frame and their lower ends set on, or more likely, in the ground just outside the horizontal logs. It is possible that the pieces of poles or planks found just outside the west wall (Fig.15) are the remains of such wall timbers. Placed close together in slanting position, they would have formed a truncated pyramid covering the platforms and the east end of the floor.

Though no remains of the roof were found it seems reasonable to assume that the central part of the room, that is the area within the rows of posts, had a cribbed roof like the Eskimo house from Nunivak Island illustrated by Collins[16]. The cribbing probably consisted of four or five tiers covered by tightly placed poles forming another flatter truncated pyramid, with a square smoke hole in the center. The whole structure, walls and roof, would have been covered over with moss turf and possibly earth. It is very likely that birch bark was also used as roofing material. Of the numerous pieces of birch bark found in and particularly outside the house, several had been stitched together to form sheets which could have been used on the roof as either patches or as a complete cover under the turf, as known from the Ingalik and the Hoyukon.[17] (fig. 17).

There can hardly be any doubt that the entrance to the main room was situated in the middle of the east wall. This is indicated by the following facts: 1) there was no sign of a platform along the east wall, 2) a 50 cm wide deep cut in the middle of the base log is probably the remains of the opening in the room, 3) the main log which forms the east side of the anteroom is heavily worn in the middle, as if stepped upon (fig. 16), 4) horizontal floor layers are present as in the main room, and some gravel wall in the anteroom, but limited to the "passage" between the two assumed entrances just mentioned.

The anteroom itself presents a problem. Except for three postholes just outside the entrance to the main room, which might indicate some structure in connection with the entrance, there was nothing in the anteroom to suggest a superstructure. The question is to what extent the anteroom was roofed. On the one hand, it is framed by heavy, horizontal logs similar to the main room, like the "passage" that connects the two assumed entrances to the house, which seems to indicate that it was roofed. On the other hand, apart from the "passage", the debris inside the frame had the same midden-like character as the fill of Field B just outside the east wall of the anteroom, with alternating layers of loose dirt and moss-turf, indicating an accumulation outside rather than inside a house. A possible solution to the problem is that

---

[16] Collins 1937: fig. 25.
[17] Clark and Clark 1974: 34 and fig. 2.

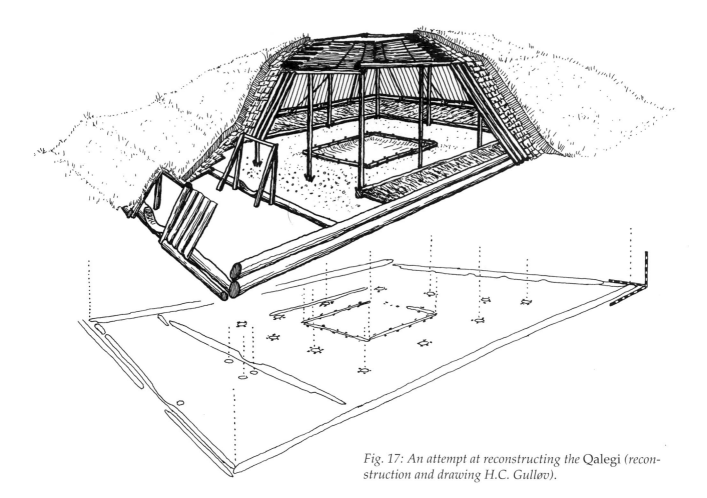

Fig. 17: An attempt at reconstructing the Qalegi *(reconstruction and drawing H.C. Gulløv).*

only a part of the anteroom was roofed and perhaps only for a period.

Whatever the explanation of the anteroom may be, it is one of several features that distinguish our house from other Ipiutak houses and suggests that it served a purpose different from ordinary houses. This is evident from the mere fact that it could hold four average Point Hope Ipiutak houses and that it would take several men to handle the timbers used in the structure. That it could have been built and occupied by several families is of course a possibility which we must not leave out of consideration, but during the entire excavation we had the feeling that this was a place where men had been working; while traces of women's activities were noticeably scarce. Weapon parts, complete, broken or unfinished, and other men's tools predominate the inventory, but what particularly impressed us was the vast amount of wood chips and shavings and pieces of wood, antler and ivory that have been worked and which made up

a major part of the floor deposit. This, in connection with the dimensions of the house and the fireplace, the 12 posts and what must have been an impressive superstructure leads me to believe that we are dealing with a men's house corresponding to the *qalegi* of the historic Eskimos of northern Alaska and the *kashgi* or *kashim* of the Eskimos and Indians further south.

In our interpretation of the house as a *qalegi* we were in full agreement with the local people who, as already mentioned, had an explanation of the mysterious "handles". Even more interesting the oldest man in the village, Qoperluk, could tell us that his father had told him that there used to be a *qalegi* in this particular place. It is possible that the mound that covered our house was the remains of a later men's house that existed in Qoperluk's father's time, though we cannot completely exclude the possibility that he was actually referring to the Ipiutak house through an old tradition that has been handed down over generations.

III. Description of the Artifacts

The great majority of implement types found in the Ipiutak house at Deering are identical with those from the Ipiutak site at Point Hope. Consequently, a detailed description of the Deering types, as well as an account of their occurrence elsewhere, will be limited to those that either do not occur in the Point Hope finds, or in one way or another differ from corresponding Ipiutak types. Regarding all identical types, reference will be made to: "Ipiutak and the Arctic Whale Hunting Culture" (Larsen & Rainey 1948), henceforth to be referred to simply as "Ipiutak".

ARCHERY

Arrowheads

The 61 arrowheads, including unclassifiable fragments, deviate in no respect from the Ipiutak arrowheads found at Point Hope. They are made of antler, the great majority decorated with four equally spaced, longitudinal lines, and with a conical, smooth tang or rather a tapering base. As at Point Hope, some of the arrowheads are furnished with ownership marks. These usually are short transverse or longitudinal lines with straight or oblique spurs. Most of the arrowheads are almost square in cross-section, like those found in the Ipiutak houses at Point Hope and not round or elliptical in cross-section like those from the burials. The cross-section depends largely on the depth of the incised, longitudinal lines.

One difference between Point Hope and Deering is worth mentioning; namely the fact that the most common type of arrowhead (type 1) at Point Hope, is represented at Deering by only one specimen, while arrowhead type 2, is much more predominant, with 15 specimens recovered. It cannot be determined whether this was a question of local preference, or whether it has something to do with differences in age of the two sites. It is not so strange that arrowhead types 1a, 2a, 4, 5, 6 and 7 do not occur in the Deering find as these are either scarce in the finds from the Ipiutak houses at Point Hope, or confined to burials as in the case of types 6 and 7.

Type 1 (Pl. 1.1).[18] As mentioned above, only one specimen of this type was found. It is shorter than any of the Point Hope specimens and is furnished with two grooves for sideblades, on opposite edges of the head and near the point.

Type 2 (Pl. 1.2),[19] is represented by 15 specimens, ranging in length from 12.4 cm to 14.7 cm. Five specimens exhibit ownership marks.

Type 3 (Pl. 1.3-5),[20] with 10 specimens, shows more variation. In fact, no two are alike, varying in their numbers of barbs and their arrangement. Of the six more or less complete specimens, one has two barbs, two have three, and three have four barbs. The barbs are typically bilateral; only one specimen has a unilateral row of barbs. In most cases the barbs are decorated with either one medial line, or with a medial and two lateral, longitudinal lines. The barbs may be awl-shaped and deeply cut as in Pl. 1.5, or low, flat ridges (Pl. 1-4). Most Type 3 arrowheads are approximately 14 cm long.

Type 8 (Pl. 1.6),[21] with 6 specimens, is more common at Deering than at Point Hope, where only five were found. They range in length from 16 to 9.5 cm and occur in two forms; one with a conical point and the other with a point which is diamond-shaped in cross section, as in the illustrated example. One specimen has an ownership mark near the tang. There are 28 fragmentary arrowheads, all of which are bases, and five have ownership marks. The number of fragmentary arrowheads is actually larger, but the remainder have been reworked and used primarily as awls. As was the case at of Point Hope, some of the tangs show thread-like impressions, probably as a result of the arrowheads having been screwed into the wooden shaft.

Arrowpoints

All 25 arrow points found at Deering belong to type 1[22]; that is with a straight base. The great majority are made of the same dark gray, partly

---

[18] Ipiutak: Pls. 1 and 32.
[19] Ipiutak: Pls 1 and 32.
[20] Ipiutak: Pls. 1 and 33.
[21] Ipiutak: Pl. 1.
[22] Ipiutak: Pls. 2 and 35.

translucent, crypto-crystalline quartz which the Eskimos at Point Hope called *angmaq*, mineralogists call chert or jasper and which we in the Ipiutak report called flint. This more or less technical term will also be used in this report. Six of the specimens are of black, silicified slate and one, Pl. 14.8, is of a dark-gray, fine-grained silicified slate. The basal end of this specimen is partly ground on both faces and is so much larger than the others (4.3 x 1.5 cm) that it may be a lance or a harpoon blade, rather than an arrow point. The smallest specimen classified as an arrow point is 2.3 x 0.8 cm. Plate 14.9 shows a specimen that is wider than the ordinary arrow points and may be a harpoon blade. Nine specimens are only partly chipped on one face, leaving part of the original flake surface untouched and on one specimen, the flake surface is visible on both sides.

Inset Blades

In the Ipiutak report, the term inset blades was used to describe blades that varied from thin asymmetrical, segment-shaped to semi lunar, bifacially chipped blades, used in arrowheads, harpoon heads, and lance heads.[23] Of 24 specimens in this category found at Deering, 18 have been classified as type 1, five as type 3, and one as type 4.

Type 1. The specimens shown in Pl. 14.10-11 represent the extremes in sizes. Both are 2 mm thick. Fifteen of the specimens are made of gray flint, two of black, silicified slate and one of chalcedony.

Type 3 (Pl. 14.12) is of chalcedony and only trimmed along the edges. The other four specimens are about the same size, bifacially chipped, and made of gray flint.

In addition to the arrow points and inset blades mentioned above, there are 21 small, unclassifiable fragments comprised of thin, bifacially chipped blades, which according to their thickness must be parts of arrow points or inset blades.

Blunt Arrowheads

Whereas the common Alaskan types of blunt

---

arrowheads, with socket or tang, are absent in the Deering find, 16 specimens were found at Ipiutak.[24] In the Ipiutak report these blunt arrowheads were classified as "implements of uncertain use, Type 1".[25] This interpretation still seems to be the best. In contrast to some of the Point Hope specimens, which were obviously made exclusively as arrowheads, all the Deering specimens are reworked and have originally served another purpose. This appears clearly from the illustrated specimens, Pl. 1.11 showing a broken-off barbed point. As with the barbed harpoon heads from Deering (Pl. 3.1-2), the point has been made into a tang. The shaft, which is pierced above the tang, has a keel-shaped point, split in the middle. An owner's mark consisting of a vertical line with two short crossbars was probably applied after its transformation into a blunt arrowhead. The specimen in Pl. 1.10 was originally a barbed prong like those in Pl. 3.13-16, and was treated the same way, except for the irregular point and traces of wear. A row of four, short transversal lines may be an ownership mark. Both specimens are of antler and decorated with incised longitudinal lines on body and barbs. In the collection there are five more blunt arrowheads made of barbed prongs, three of antler and two of ivory. One of the antler specimens is decorated with fine lines and triangular dots. The rest are without barbs and made of weapon shafts of antler, for instance arrowheads and harpoon fore-shafts or blanks of such shafts. Only three of them are perforated. Four specimens have incised lines as seen in Pl. 1.12-13, five have a keel-shaped point, one specimen has screw-like impressions on the tang, and one has an ownership mark consisting of three, short transversal lines. The specimens of this type ranged in length from 5.1 to 12 cm.

Arrow Shafts

The collection contains 74 broken wooden shafts, at least some of which must be arrow shafts. They range in diameter from 1.2 to 0.8 cm, which is the same as more than a score of Eskimo arrow shafts from Alaska, Canada, and Greenland in the National Museum of Denmark. However, we cannot be absolutely certain that all 74 specimens are arrow shafts because as we shall see later, shafts

---

[23] Ipiutak: 66 and 98, Pls. 2 and 36.
[24] Ipiutak,: Pl. 1.20-21.
[25] Ipiutak: 67 and Pl. 28.1-7.

for bird spears as well as some harpoons have the same average diameter. Unfortunately, all the fragments are middle sections, otherwise a notch in the base or a socket for a head would have given the answer to their identity. The shafts are made from a much thicker piece of straight-grown spruce and most of them are remarkably well made, round and smooth as if they were made on a lathe, though a magnifying glass reveals that they have been trimmed with a stone scraper. A few of them show traces of red paint and one specimen (Pl. 4.12), in addition to being painted red, has two 3 mm wide, black, transverse bands.

Of 37 thin, round shafts at least 12 must be interpreted as toy arrow shafts on account of their size and because they have the characteristic notch in the end (Pl. 1.14). Three of them are also complete with a hole, or a slit for the arrowhead in the other end; one still has remnants of thin baleen lashing. The three complete specimens range in length from 23.5 to 18.5 cm and in thickness from 0.6 to 0.4 cm. The longest fragmentary shaft is 39.7 cm with a diameter of 0.7 cm. One specimen shows traces of red paint.

Arrow Straightener

Plate 4.14 is an arrow straightener or a blank for one. It cannot be decided whether it is of a preparatory stage, or has been used as is. It is made of an unworked, 22 cm long antler prong in which a hole has been roughly gouged out. The only specimen of this kind found at Point Hope is of ivory and has a smooth, decorated surface[26].

Bows

The collection contains two fragments of what seems to have been bows for adults; one (Pl. 1.7) is of birch and the other is of spruce. However both of them are too incomplete to tell us anything about how this type of bow was used by the occupants of the house. For the answer to this we must turn to the toy bows, of which twelve specimens

were found (Pl. 1.8-9). They are all made of spruce and all in fragments. None of them are much more than half their original length. They vary considerably in size, though three fragments of about similar size are estimated to have been about 40 cm long when they were complete. They seem to belong to one type of bow, viz. a straight bow with flat "wings", and a thicker, rounded, and narrower grip. In most cases one side of the bow, presumably the back, is flat while the other side is slightly rounded. The only noticeable variation is in the width of the wings.

The same form occurred at Ipiutak[27] and was common in historical times among the Alaskan Eskimo south of Norton Sound[28]. Though none of our specimens had backing, there are indications on two that backing was used. One of the specimens (Pl. 1.9) has three oblique notches on each side below the nock, and the other has a pair of notches just below the nock. Even if these toy bows did not have backing, it is possible that the real bows had similar notches and that they served as support for a backing. In that case a "Southern" backing would have been most likely.

Bow guards

Among the "implements of uncertain use" from the Ipiutak site at Point Hope were five spool-shaped objects of antler classified as Type 0 (Ipiutak: Pl. 28, 26-27) and tentatively interpreted as "wrist guards" of the particular kind that attach to the middle of certain Athapaskan bows[29]. Three specimens from Deering were undoubtedly used for the same purpose, though slightly different in shape and made from walrus ivory. Plate 1.17 shows the closest resemblance to the specimens from Point Hope. The other two are flattened and have a slightly curved stem, with a simple line decoration, a concave plate at one end and either one or two holes in the other end (Pl. 1.15-16). They range in length from 3.6 to 3.8 cm. If the interpretation of these specimens is correct, and I believe it is, then the holes were used to fasten this guard to the middle of the belly of the bow with sinew-thread or a skin throng. The concave plate intercepted the bowstring when it was released, thereby prevented the wrist from being hit.

Because so few specimens of this artifact oc-

[26] Ipiutak: Pl. 42.14.
[27] Ipiutak: Pl. 31.1-3.
[28] Murdoch 1885: Pl. I-III.
[29] Ipiutak: 68.

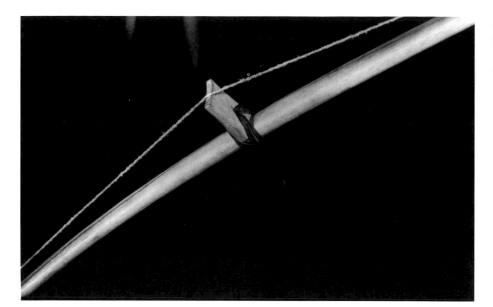

Fig. 18: Bow with "hand guard" from White River, Yukon (photo Frederick Johnson).

curred in the large Ipiutak find from Point Hope, it was assumed that this kind of bow attachment was not in common use[30]. Now with three specimens from one house, we must revise this statement, at least as far as Deering Ipiutak is concerned. The difference in shape between the Deering specimens and those from Point Hope may indicate a difference in age between the two finds, or local variation.

More significant is the limited distribution of this form of wrist protection in connection with archery. With only one known exception outside the Ipiutak culture, bow guards are only known from the Northern Athapaskans. These were made of wood and generally larger than those of the Ipiutak culture (fig. 18). The use of bow guards are recorded from most of the Athapaskan groups in Alaska, namely Ingalik,[31] Tanaina,[32] Tanana,[33] Chandalar,[34] Crow River Kutchins,[35] Han,[36] Ahtena[37] and outside Alaska they are

known from Tuchone,[38] Kaska,[39] Dogrib,[40] and Great Bear Lake Indians.[41] Though I have been unable to find references to its occurrence among the Koyukon, Nabesna, and Hare, there can hardly be any doubt that bow guards at one time were used by at least all Athapaskans in Alaska and possibly by all the northern Athapaskans. As shown above, we have evidence as far east as Great Slave Lake, and the fact that a bow with two bow guards is known from the Haida,[42] the only example I have found outside Athapaskan territory, indicates that bow guards were also used in the southern part of the territory as well.

SEA MAMMAL HUNTING

Harpoon heads

With a few exceptions, harpoon heads from Deering are identical with the Ipiutak harpoon heads from Point Hope; hence a detailed description will be limited to those that occur for the first time.

Type 1. (Pl. 2.1-4)[43] Of the four specimens, numbers 1-2 are of antler and the other two of bone. Each has three spurs and an awl-shaped point; the only difference is that the bone specimens are stubbier, and have fewer decorative longitudinal lines than those made of antler. Plate 2.2 is exceptional, in that the grooves above the line hole usually intended for sideblades are too narrow and

[30] Ipiutak: 68.
[31] Woldt 1884: 193.
[32] Osgood 1937: Pl. 8 A-B.
[33] McKennan 1959: fig. 5 K.L.
[34] McKennan 1959: 52.
[35] Osgood 1936: 72.
[36] Jones 1867: 324.
[37] Allen 1887: Pl. 17.
[38] Da Nat. Mus. Cat. No. H.b. l08.
[39] Honigman 1954: 35.
[40] A.J. Mason 1946: Pl. 3F.
[41] Osgood 1932: 61.
[42] Am. Mus. Nat. Hist. New York.
[43] Ipiutak: Pl. 3.1-18.

a   b

shallow to hold blades and here are only ornamental. This form did not occur at Point Hope, and the fact that the grooves are merely vestigial might indicate that this form is later than the ordinary type. This specimen was found in the second layer in the house.

Type 2. (Pl. 2. 5-7)[44] As it appears from the illustrations the three specimens – each made of antler – are different in shape. Number 5 corresponds somewhat in size, shape and decoration to the Ipiutak specimen, Pl. 4.1. And, like Ipiutak Pl. 4.3, it has a crack that has been repaired with a lashing fixed in a transversal groove. Specimen no. 6 is quite refined in shape and decoration (see fig. 19a) and has no true counterpart in the Point Hope collection; the closest being Ipiutak Pl. 4.14-15, which also resembles the third Deering specimen.

Type 3.[45] Both specimens of this type (Pl. 2.8-9) are of antler and have an awl-shaped point. They differ in the number of spurs (no. 8 has four and no. 9 has two) and the fact that no. 9 is decorated in typical Ipiutak style (fig. 19b) while no. 8 is undecorated. In form they resemble the Ipiutak specimens Pl. 5. 8-10. The collection also contains four blanks, presumably of this type.

Rare forms. Plate 2.10 is from the fifth layer of the house, and is mounted in normal respects. It is of bone, has a closed shaft socket with one spur, a low-lying barb and above that, a groove for a sideblade. The line hole is oblong and narrow and the point flattened. This form is unknown at Point Hope, though the oblong line hole, the low barb, and the blade slot at right angles to the line hole are reminiscent of certain harpoon heads from the near Ipiutak burials[46] though no single specimen has all the features mentioned.

Pl. 2.11, is from the house's first layer and is a blank that lacks only the line hole and the socket. It is made of antler and resembles an Ipiutak harpoon head type 3, except for the fact that it is furnished with a small barb on each side of the line hole position and as with Pl. 2.2, it has rudimentary blade slots above the line hole. The point is diamond shaped in cross-section and the base has five more or less pronounced spurs. The specimen is unique and for the time being must be considered a local variant.

Miniature forms. There are two miniature harpoon heads in the collection. Plate 2.12 is made of antler and, except for the lack of line hole and grooves for sideblades, resembles type 1. Plate 2.13 is of wood, has a closed shaft socket and resembles type 3, except for the absence of blade slots.

Barbed Harpoon Heads. The two long, slender barbed heads represent a new Ipiutak type. The one barbed harpoon head that was found in an Ipiutak burial at Point Hope is much heavier and has unilateral barbs.[47] The Deering specimens have bilateral barbs and are much more elegant, particularly Pl. 3.1 which is a very fine example of Ipiutak craftsmanship. This has two staggered barbs on each side and on the longitudinal axis there is a deeply incised, narrow groove that connects the blade slit with the small, oblong line hole. On the base end, there is a rather flat, tapering tang (Pl. 3.2), which has only three barbs, and is less carefully made. Another shallow, longitudinal groove has been applied along one side and it is not quite straight. It is furnished with a chipped, lanceolate end blade of black, siliceous slate.

In addition to the complete specimens there are two fragmentary ones. These are both front parts, each with a slit for a blade. One is 9.2 cm long, and has a barb with a decorative, medial line. The

---

44 Ipiutak: Pl. 4.
45 Ipiutak: Pl. 5.1-10.
46 Ipiutak: Pl. 78.5-7 and Pl. 84.9-11.
47 Ipiutak: Pl. 42.10.

  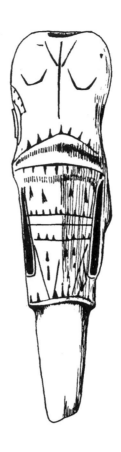

Fig. 20: Harpoon socket piece, approx. 6 cm long (drawing J. Rosing).).

other is a shorter specimen, lacks barbs and has more elaborate decoration with plain and spurred lines. The classification of the latter as a barbed harpoon head is doubtful. The form of barbed harpoon heads described above seems to be unique.

Harpoon End Blades

Five bifacially chipped points of chert and silicified slate (Pl. 2.16-18) have been tentatively classified as harpoon end blades. Three of them are fragmentary and two are less symmetrical than the specimens from Point Hope.[48]

Harpoon Socket Pieces

The only harpoon socket piece in the collection (Pl. 2.14) corresponds to socket piece type 1, in the

---

[48] Ipiutak: Pl. 2. 34-39.
[49] Ipiutak: Pl. 6.1 and 38.1-3.
[50] Ipiutak: Pl. 25.1.

Ipiutak collection from Point Hope.[49] This is made of antler, round in cross-section, has a 6.5 mm wide and 9 mm deep, round shaft socket and a conical tang. Above the tang is a narrow, oblong hole for lashing the socket to the wooden shaft. Contrary to most Point Hope specimens of this type, which are carved to represent animal heads, this specimen represents a human head with contorted features (see fig. 20). In this, as in other respects, it resembles the carving of a human head from Point Hope,[50] and it thus confirms our tentative identification of this head as a socket piece.

Actually, the decoration of the Deering specimen shows two human faces; namely a primary motif in relief and on the reverse side, a large mouth, two incised carved lines representing eyes and between them a tridental design representing the second figure's nose. The eyes of the second head are two round sockets with wooden inserts, with a hole in the middle. As it appears from fig. 19, most of the surface is covered with spurred and plain, incised lines and isolated triangular dots, forming a not very accurate pattern. The use of triangular dots either isolated or attached to incised lines, is quite common in the Ipiutak find from Point Hope. As a close resemblance, I may refer to the ornamental band illustrated in the Ipiutak publication fig. 43.

Harpoon Foreshafts

Fifteen specimens of antler and one of walrus ivory have been interpreted as harpoon foreshafts. Classification into types is not as simple as was the case with the foreshafts from Point Hope. There we had two definite types, a short form (type 1) which was used with socket pieces[51], and a long form (type 2) which we presumed had been attached directly to the harpoon shaft.[52] In other words, type 1 is a detachable foreshaft and type 2 is a fixed foreshaft.

In our collection from Deering there are several short foreshafts, but none that with certainty may be called detachable, though Pl. 2.19 is almost identical with the Point Hope specimen illustrated in the Ipiutak report Pl. 6.3. One reason I only classify a few of the Deering specimens as type 1, is because none of them have the short, almost cylindrical base which is characteristic of several of the Point Hope specimens of this type. Another reason is that only three out of the ten foreshafts have the medially placed, small, oblong line hole that occurs on all type 1 specimens from Point Hope, and which is essential to detachable foreshafts.

Using the line hole as a criterion, we have in our collection three harpoon foreshafts of type 1. One is Pl. 2.19, with a wedged-shaped base and longitudinal, incised lines on three sides extending from the line hole to the broken point. The second is also a base end fragment, of a similar specimen, but with a slightly longer tang, while the third is a weathered specimen that has two rectangular line holes, similar to the Point Hope specimen, Pl. 38. 1. On this third specimen the base is broken, but it seems to have been conical.

Thirteen foreshafts in the collection have been classified as type 2, on the supposition that they were fixed, though they are generally much shorter than the harpoon foreshafts of type 2 from

Point Hope. The longest specimen and the one which most resembles those from Point Hope is Pl. 2.22. It is of walrus ivory, round in cross-section, with four equally spaced, longitudinal lines, and medial slots near the base (compare to Ipiutak: Pl. 39). The others, made of antler, range in length from 13.2 cm (Pl. 2. 23) to 7.6 cm. Most of them are spindle-shaped and six are decorated with longitudinal lines. In most cases, the base is wedge-shaped or flattened, and the point is conical; only two specimens have a flat point made to receive an open-socketed harpoon head.

The classification of two of the specimens is questionable, in so far as they may actually have been used as detachable foreshafts. Plate. 2.20 is the size and shape of a type 1 foreshaft, but lacks the line hole; yet it has a slight groove around the middle that would fit a line or string, by which it could have been attached to the harpoon line. It has a flat base and a round point. Plate 2.21 has the same shape of base and point as the previous piece, and it has an oblong hole near the base for attachment to the harpoon line.

As at Point Hope, a number of common and characteristic elements of Eskimo harpooning are absent, namely finger rests, float mouthpieces, float bars, and wood plugs. At Point Hope the absence of the wooden objects may be explained by the poor preservation of such material, but this explanation does not apply to Deering where wood was excellently preserved. The Deering find thus confirms our previous assumption that the Ipiutak people did not use floats with their harpoons. As mentioned in the Ipiutak report, the absence of floats also excludes whaling, in its arctic form. For the sake of completeness, it should be added that no whaling harpoon gear was as found at Deering.

OTHER HUNTING AND FISHING GEAR

Lance heads

In the collection there are eleven fragments that may be identified as parts of lance heads or daggers, of the types described from Point Hope.[53] They are all of walrus ivory and all but one, which has a perforated base, have grooves for insert blades, on one or both sides. Of the four illus-

---

[51] Ipiutak: Pl. 6.2 and Pl. 38.1, 2, 4 and 5.
[52] Ipiutak: Pl. 39.1-5.
[53] Ipiutak, Pl. 6. 9-12, Pl. 40 and 41.

trated specimens, Pl. 3.6 with two slots for side blades, has a conical, unperforated base and should accordingly be classified as an Ipiutak lance head, type 2[54]. Like type 1, Pl. 3.7 has an oblong perforation near the base and its lower part is decorated with thin, parallel lines. Plate 3.8 is a blank, with six opposite blade grooves. The small fragment Pl. 3.9 is the only specimen with decoration typical of the Ipiutak lance heads and daggers, namely a pattern of both coarse and fine parallel lines and a circle[55]. The incised lines show traces of red paint.

Bird darts

It was suggested in the Ipiutak report that the Ipiutak people had two kinds of bird darts. One has an end prong and three side prongs, and was probably adopted from the Okvik culture; the other kind has multiple, usually slightly curved end prongs which we considered the original Ipiutak type[56]. The Deering excavation seems to confirm this supposition. As at Point Hope, more or less curved end prongs are far more numerous than side prongs, of which there are only one set of three and two questionable, fragmentary specimens. In addition, the Deering find contains no less than 23 front sections of wooden shafts for bird darts. These are with multiple end prongs, indicating that it is a common type and that bird hunting played an important role at the time the Deering house was occupied. In this connection, it is worth mentioning that E. W. Nelson in his description of bird darts writes that they were used primarily in late summer and fall "when geese and ducks have molted their wing-feathers and are unable to fly", and that they are also used for catching various, young water fowl.[57] Additionally, one of the natives from Deering volunteered the interesting information that they used to have two kinds of bird darts; one with end prong and three side prongs for use at sea, and one with three end prongs which they used on

rivers. His explanation for having two kinds was that the latter was more practical in shallow water whereas the former easily became stuck in the river bottom.

End prongs (Pl. 3.13-16). The Ipiutak collection from Point Hope contained 48 barbed prongs which we interpreted as either end prongs for bird darts or leister prongs.[58] As mentioned above, the interpretation of these as prongs for use as bird darts rather than fish spears is now substantiated by the presence in the Deering find of the wooden shafts in which they undoubtedly were inserted, and which are virtually identical with bird dart shafts used in Alaska in historical time.[59]

With 68 specimens, including fragments and blanks, end prongs are by far the most common weapon part found at Deering, a rather surprising fact. Of these, 56 are of antler and 18 of walrus ivory, while at Point Hope there were slightly more of ivory than of antler. The complete specimens range in length from 20.1 to 29.3 cm and have an average thickness of 0.8 cm. Usually they are slightly curved and with very few exceptions, furnished with one to four longitudinal, incised lines. The shaft body is round or elliptical in cross-section, and the tang is conical or flattened. There is considerable variation in the number and arrangement of barbs, which usually are long and slender and only slightly protruding. They may be unilateral or bilateral, the latter being the more common. In one instance, Pl. 3.15, the barbs have a medial, incised line, as on the barbs of some of the type 3 Ipiutak arrowheads. The three oblique lines and one horizontal line seen on Pl. 3.15 are probably an owner's mark, a trait this specimen shares with a few other end prongs.

Wooden shafts for bird darts. The collection contains 22 wooden shafts, which by their shape may be identified as front sections of bird darts. The shafts that are made of spruce are perfectly round in cross-section, 1 cm thick at the lower end, and increasing in thickness to an average of 17 cm near the point. An exceptionally heavy specimen is 2.1 cm thick. Three specimens are claviform like Pl. 4.1, while the majority has a conical point like Pl. 4.2-4. The decisive feature is three evenly spaced, longitudinal grooves near the point in which the prongs have been inserted. Marks from the lashing that held the prongs in place are visible on 8 specimens. Some specimens like Pl. 4.3-4,

[54] Ipiutak, Pl. 40. 9-13.
[55] Ipiutak: fig. 40.
[56] Ipiutak: 78.
[57] Nelson 1899:152
[58] Ipiutak: Pl. 7.11-16 and Pl. 42.1-2.
[59] Nelson 1899: Pl. LIX, 1-6.

have a collar, a groove, or a slight protrusion near the point to secure the lashing, which may have been of sinew, skin, or more likely, of willow or spruce roots (comp. Pl. 6). Eight specimens show traces of red paint, and it is very likely that all of them were red at the time they were used, just as weapon shafts in the Bering Sea region were painted in historical time. The shape of the grooves of the best-preserved specimen (Pl. 4.3) indicates that prongs with a conical tang were used in this particular shaft and experiments with insertion of prongs show that originally they must have bent outwards.

In addition to the front sections, there are 26 bird dart shaft ends. They are identifiable by a low, round depression in the end, which shows that they have been used in connection with a throwing board with a peg in the end. They are made of spruce, are completely round in cross-section, and most of them taper slightly toward the rear where in order to give room for the depression, they again become thicker. Plate 4.5 is the longest specimen. It is 1.1 cm thick at the front, tapering to 0.9 cm and then thickens to 1.0 cm at the base itself. Other specimens in the collection have a more pronounced expansion of the base. A lashing of split roots remains on Pl. 4.6.

Undoubtedly there are several bird dart shaft midsections in the collection, but those are indistinguishable from arrow shafts.

Side prongs for bird dart

In addition to a bird dart with end prongs, we also have evidence of the use of side prongs; namely one complete set of side prongs and two fragmentary specimens which may tentatively be interpreted as such. All five specimens are made from walrus ivory. The three side prongs illustrated in Pl. 3.3-5 were found together, stuck into the south wall of the main room. This, in connection with their identical shape, size and material of partly fossilized walrus ivory, left no doubt that they belonged to the same bird dart. The stem is square in cross-section, the tang is flat, and the points apparently resharpened. They have been secured

to the shaft with two lashings, one through the holes and the other through the notch on the back of the tang. The two partly fossilized ivory fragments have a flat, pointed tang, an oblong line hole and one barb on the inside.

In order to hold the side prongs, this type of bird dart must have had a much heavier shaft than those described above. It was also probably furnished with one heavy end prong. In the collection there are a few fragments of heavy weapon points with two barbs that might be end prongs for this type of bird dart, but they are too incomplete for a definite identification.

As already stated, the Deering find has shown the importance in the Ipiutak culture of the bird dart with multiple end prongs as compared to bird darts with side prongs. This supports the supposition expressed in the Ipiutak report that the former is the original Ipiutak type, and the latter an adaptation from the Neo-Eskimo culture. The fact that the bird dart with multiple end prongs has wide distribution also outside the Eskimo area, while the form with side prongs is a particular Eskimo type, also indicates that the former is the older of the two. This was pointed out by Birket-Smith as early as 1929.[60]

Throwing sticks

The finding of four front sections of throwing sticks (Pl. 4.15-18) verifies the tentative identification of a doubtful specimen from Point Hope.[61] The Point Hope specimen, complete except for the peg in the upper end, is 46.3 cm long and has a simple handle without any indentations or holes for the fingers.

The Deering specimens are made of spruce and are more slender than any Eskimo throwing sticks. Plate 4.15 is the most elaborate, and a fine example of the Ipiutak craftsman's ability to carve in wood. As it appears from the photograph and the drawing, fig. 21, it ends in an animal head that mostly resembles a seal head. A round peg of walrus ivory has been inserted as one of the eyes, while only the socket remains of the other. Five smaller ivory pegs probably imitate teeth and there is a similar peg in each cheek. The pupil of the eye is inserted with a tiny plug of unidentified organic material. In cross-section this forms a

[60] Birket-Smith, 1929 (II): 65.
[61] Ipiutak: 77, Pl. 31.9.

Fig. 21: Throwing stick with animal features, 13 cm long (drawing J. Rosing).

black ring, surrounding a sickle-shaped, white spot with a hole in the middle. Twenty-four similar plugs, each 1 mm in diameter and 4 mm long, are placed symmetrically on the back of the head, 12 on each side. Eighteen of them outline a 4.5 cm long, slightly curved slot, which does not seem to serve any practical purpose. On the back of the head is a 3.9 cm long and 0.5 cm deep groove that may be purely ornamental or may have served some unknown purpose. On the underside are a groove for the weapon shaft and a 1 cm deep socket for an oblong peg.

Plate 4.18 is even more slender than the one just described and similarly ends in an animal head; see fig 22. The groove for the weapon shaft is less pronounced and instead of an inserted peg it has a small knob that fits the socket in the end of the bird dart shafts. The remaining two specimens, Pl. 4.16 and 17, are not decorated and judging from a wide lashing groove near the end, they must have had some sort of peg lashed on. The threads of baleen which may be seen on Pl. 4.17 are probably remains of the lashing.

From the size and shape of the Ipiutak throwing sticks, it seems obvious that they were used for bird darts with three end prongs. Likewise, they were probably also used with harpoons, some of which had shafts as slender as those for bird darts.

Miscellaneous weapon shafts

Wooden shafts for arrows and bird darts have already been mentioned, but in addition to these there are 16 front sections of wooden shafts, with sockets for insertion of weapon points or a socket pieces. The specimen, Pl. 2.15, illustrated with the harpoon socket piece attached (Pl. 2.14) has a 3.5 cm deep, squarish opening 1.2 cm wide, into which a socket piece similar to that shown in Pl. 2.14 could fit. Given the dimensions, the shaft may be for a light harpoon. The shaft is only 1.0 cm thick where broken off; that is no thicker than an arrow shaft. Traces of a spiral binding cover the entire surface. A peculiar feature that may be seen in the illustration and which I am unable to explain, is that a small, rectangular piece has been cut out of the side of the socket and put back in place. A hole of the same size and shape occurs at the same place on another, similar shaft (Pl. 4.8), so it has served some purpose. The socket on this specimen is cruciform, and too small to hold a harpoon socket piece. However plate 4.11 may well have held a socket piece the size of Pl. 2.14. Plate 4.9 is probably also a harpoon shaft. Plate 4.10 is 2.5 cm in diameter and probably held a lance head or a heavy end prong for a bird spear of the type furnished with side prongs. Eight middle sections of similarly heavy shafts may be parts

Fig. 22: Throwing stick with animal features, 16.2 cm long (drawing J. Rosing).

of shafts for harpoons, lances, or bird spears. The incised X on Pl. 4.13 may be an ownership mark.

Four fragmentary shafts are similar to Pl. 4.7 in size and shape, and have probably been used for the same kind of weapon. The sockets are 3 to 3.5 cm deep, have an oblong opening, and each has a narrow collar to support a binding at the upper end. The only weapon heads in the collection with a flat tang that would fit these sockets are the barbed harpoon heads, although they seem rather heavy for slender shafts. In addition to the shafts just mentioned, there are four fragments of front sections of shafts with a collar at the end.

Snare parts

In a later section, I will return to the small bird bone tubes with notches or a transverse groove in one end, which were described in the Ipiutak report as "implements of uncertain use, type 3" and interpreted as parts of ground squirrel snares.[62] For now, it is worthwhile to note that another common type of artifact at Point Hope, which was also interpreted as a snare part,[63] does not occur in the Deering find.

Salmon spears

The Deering find yielded the first complete salmon spear head consisting of five parts, a center prong, two side prongs, and two barbs. The five piece assembly (Pl. 3.12) which is typical of Ipiutak culture,[64] was found together in a test pit west of the house, but so close that we may safely include them in the find from the house. Two almost complete specimens were also found inside the house, namely Pl. 3.11 of which the tip of the prongs and the barbs are missing, and another with broken prongs, but with the barbs preserved. As seen in the illustrated specimen (Pl. 3, 10), the side prong has no lashing slot, but instead a knob on the back to secure the lashing. This is an unusual feature otherwise only known from the Ipiutak material excavated by Campbell at Anaktuvuk Pass.[65] The great difference in size between P. 3.11 and 3.12 is worth noticing, and the latter is not even the largest. Of six additional prongs found in the house, one side prong is 20.7 cm long, 2 cm longer than those illustrated. All the salmon spear components in the collection are made of antler, and all, except for the barbs mentioned above, conform to the same general pattern. Five of the prongs are decorated with the characteristic four longitudinal lines.

MEANS OF TRANSPORTATION

In my opinion, the most significant finds from the Deering site are those connected with transporta-

[62] Ipiutak: 79 and Pl. 28.12-14.
[63] Ipiutak: 79 and Pl. 28.8-11.
[64] Ipiutak: 78 and PL. 7. 7-24.
[65] Campbell 1959: fig 3 j-k.

Fig. 23: (clockwise) Sled runner (P7361), snowshoe frame piece (P7357), arrowhead (P7972), snowbeater? (P7632), snowbeater? (P7372) and barbed harpoon head (P7926). Scale approx. 1:7 (photo L. Larsen).

occur for the first time, this subject will be dealt with at greater length than others.

Sleds

As just mentioned, the occurrence of sleds in the Ipiutak culture was anticipated, but the type of sled from the Deering find came as a surprise. One might expect a simple, low runner sled or one built-up with arches as described by Ford from Birnirk,[67] but although we did not find sufficient material to make a complete reconstruction of the Ipiutak sled, we had enough to show that it was a built-up sled of a type hitherto not found in Alaska.

The incomplete picture we are able to provide of the Ipiutak sled is based on the largest and best preserved piece of a runner (fig. 23) found in the third floor-layer of the house, and four more or less complete toy sled runners (Pl. 5. 9-12). The large runner is made of spruce and is 89 cm long, 7.1 cm wide in front and 4.6 cm in the rear end. The runner is 2.4 cm thick just back of the raised part -which we refer to as a stanchion. In front and along the left side of the runner it is 1.9 cm thick, tapering off toward the right side to form a sharp edge. This edge is the result of wear and shows that we are dealing with a left runner. The stanchion is a characteristic feature and integral part of the runner, and is approximately 12 cm long, 5 cm wide at the base and 4.6 cm at the top, it was placed 28 cm from the rear of the runner, measured from the middle of the transversal hole. The rectangular hole on the top of the stanchion is 1.7 cm long, 1.0 cm wide, and 1.4 cm deep. A similar hole is found on other stanchions in the collection (Pl. 6. 12-13) and they are meant for insertion of a dowel, the other end of which fits into a corresponding hole in an extension piece, like that seen in Pl. 6.9 (see fig. 24). The only complete stanchion in the collection, Pl. 6.11 is 11.5 cm high, and if this depicts a standard height it meant that the stanchion on our largest runner has had a 6 cm high

tion. In the Ipiutak report, it was assumed that the Ipiutak people used both sleds and boats, but except for a few flat wooden boards which we thought could be sled shoes, the Point Hope site yielded nothing that could substantiate our assumption[66]. However, thanks to the exceptionally good conditions for preservation of wood at Deering, we found similar wooden boards and other parts of sleds. Indecently, the wooden boards turned out not to be sled shoes but sled runners. We also found definite proof of the knowledge of boats and unexpectedly, several pieces of snowshoes. Due to the importance of transportation in Eskimo culture and to the fact that most of the Deering artifacts in this category

---

[66] Ipiutak:147.

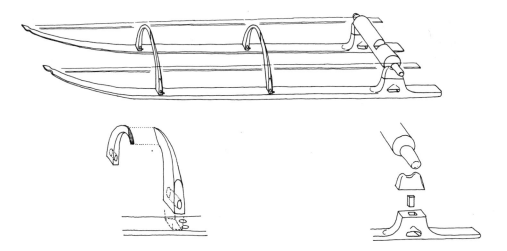

Fig. 24: An attempt at recon-
structing (by Keld Jessen
Hansen) the Deering sled
(drawing H.C. Gulløv).

extension. Forty-five cm in front of the middle of
the stanchion are two vertical holes which on the
underside are connected by a groove, as shown on
fig. 24. This illustration also shows the wear on
the runner and that the sliding surface is the tangent plane of the wood. The runner seems to be
complete except for the missing extension of the
stanchion and the front part, which is broken off.

Having learnt from the largest and the most
well preserved piece of the sled, let us now turn to
the runners of toy sleds. The largest and most
complete of these is made of willow wood and
illustrated in Pl. 5.12. It is 34 cm long, 2.2 cm wide
and 1.5 cm thick near the stanchion, which is also
1.7 cm wide and 1.5 cm high. The front of the runner is considerably thinner than the rest; only 0.4
cm near the point. A slight thinning of the upper
surface is noticeable 11 cm from the point, but is
mostly apparent on the sliding surface, beginning
9 cm from the point. The runner tapers slightly
toward the point, which is furnished with a notch
on each side. The thinning of the front part that is
also distinct on another toy runner (Pl. 5.10)
undoubtedly indicates that the front part of the
runners was bent upwards. The toy runners may
also give us an idea of the original length of our
largest runner. Assuming that the toy sled runners
are made to an approximate scale, from the position of the stanchion on the toy runner (Pl. 5.12) in
relation to the total length of the runner, I calcu-
late the original length of the large runner to
approximately 1.60 m.

In addition to the two runners described the
find contains 53 wooden pieces that have been

interpreted as parts of sleds, all made of spruce.
Plate 5.6 is a section of a runner of approximately
the same width and thickness as the largest runner. Both ends are missing and only the basis of
the stanchion remains. The runner in Pl. 5.7 is 5.6
cm wide and broken off at both ends. While the
right side is 1.7 cm thick the left side is quite thin
indicating that it is a right runner. The transversal
perforation of the stanchion has the form of a 3 cm
long, horizontal slit. Plate 5.8 shows the underside
of a section of a right runner broken off at both
ends and with distinct marks of wear from friction. Not illustrated are 6 small fragments of runners, easily identified by the wear on the sliding
surface, which is always on the tangent plane of
the wood.

Plate 5.5 shows five out of nine front runner
fragments, identified by the wear through friction
on one side and the notches at the end, as seen on
the toy runners, Pl. 5.10 and 12. They vary in
width from 3.9 cm (Pl. 5.1) to 5.6 cm (not illustrated) and are all about 1 cm thick. Most of them
are bent upwards and have simple notches like Pl.
5.3-5. One more has probably had double notches
as in Pl. 5.1-2. Similar end pieces of runners occur
in the collection from the Ipiutak site at Point
Hope that is now in the National Museum. The
find contains 28 pieces of stanchions ranging from
a complete specimen, Pl. 6.11, to thin slivers easily
recognizable as sections of stanchions. As mentioned above, Pl. 6.11 is 11.5 cm high and 4.8 cm
wide at the base and 4.3 cm at the top. The surface
on top is concave, indicating that the crosspiece,
which undoubtedly rested in this hollow, had a

rounded surface. There are 10 top-pieces of stanchions, Pl. 6. 4-8 and 16, all with the same wide, transverse groove, some deeper (Pl. 6.5), others shallower like Pl. 6.16. Of the ten, three have been fastened to the rest of the stanchion with a dowel inserted in a rectangular hole in the bottom (Pl. 6.9). They vary in size from 3.8 x 5.7 cm (Pl. 6.7) to 4.8 x 7.7 cm (Pl. 6.16). Of the basal parts of stanchions, Pl. 6.14 seems to be unfinished. The other illustrated specimens, Pl. 6.12, 13 and 15 are very carefully executed and show little variation in shape and size. It is worthy to note that in shaping the curved front and backside of the stanchion, where the craftsman had to cut against the grain, he has used a beaver-tooth knife. As seen on the illustrations, three specimens have had an extension. The apparent frequent use of stanchion extensions may be due to repairs, but it could also be a result of a scarcity of wood of sufficient thickness.

The three curved pieces, Pl. 6.1-3, are probably arches similar to those used in many built-up sleds in Alaska and in the northeastern region of Asia. These are made of spruce and rather uniform in shape and dimensions. The lower part, which is more or less quadrangular in cross section, has an oblong, longitudinal perforation 1.5 to 2.5 cm above the flat base, which was undoubtedly used for a lashing. Above the line hole the cross section becomes triangular. All three pieces are broken in the distal end so it cannot be determined whether they originally consisted of one piece or two pieces somehow connected in the middle (fig. 24) Assuming that they are part of an arch, their purpose has been to connect the two runners. Our largest runner has, as mentioned, two perforations 45 cm from the stanchion and it is most likely that an arch was placed there. This was secured by a lashing fitted through the two holes which were countersunk on the underside to protect the lashing from friction (fig. 24). One should have expected to find some indication of an attachment of an arch on the presumably complete toy sled runners, Pl. 5.10 and 12, but that is not the case. Plate. 5.11, however, seems to have had something in the place where an arch should

have been situated. Unfortunately, the fourth toy runner, Pl. 5.9, has been cut in the critical place. We do not have conclusive evidence of the use of arches in connection with the Ipiutak sleds, but considering that the hitherto earliest known sleds from Northwest Alaska had them, namely from the Birnirk and Thule cultures[68], there is good reason to believe that we are right in our interpretation of the three pieces.

The two runners must of course also have been connected at the stanchions, but we do not know for sure what the connecting piece was like. All we know is that the ends must have been rounded to fit the concave top of the stanchions. The only piece of wood in the collection, which could have served as a crosspiece is illustrated in Pl. 8. 8. It is roughly rounded and has a total length of 47.3 cm. The center part is 6 cm thick, the ends 3.4 and 4 cm thick respectively. As it appears from the illustration, there is a wide, deep cut almost in the center and a more shallow and narrow cut at right angles to it; but whether or not they have served a function in connection with a sled is uncertain. On the whole, the piece in question is so crudely made that if it was used as part of a sled, it was presumably as only makeshift repair.

What conclusions can we draw from the sled-parts described above, regarding the type of sled used by the people of the Ipiutak culture? For one thing, we can say that it was a built-up sled, and to my knowledge the earliest occurrence so far of this type of sled in the New World. The built-up sled has its main distribution in the Old World where it has presumably existed since the Stone Age.[69] The earliest finds are runners found in bogs in Sweden, Finland, and West Siberia. These runners are flat, generally longer and wider than ours, and have holes in the upper surface into which posts have been mortised. In later finds from the same regions, there are flat runners of the same width as ours. The special and very characteristic trait of our runner – the stanchion carved out of the same piece of wood as the whole runner is also known from Sweden, but from historic times. It occurs for example on a "timber-sledge" from Åsele in Västerbotten, now in Nordiska Museet in Stockholm. [70] Oddly enough, we find the same feature as far to the east of Alaska as Sweden is to the west; namely from Labrador. The toy or model sled from Ungava Bay collected by

[67] Ford 1959:152.
[68] Ford 1959: figs. 77c and 76a.
[69] Berg 1935.
[70] Berg 1935: Pl. XI.2.

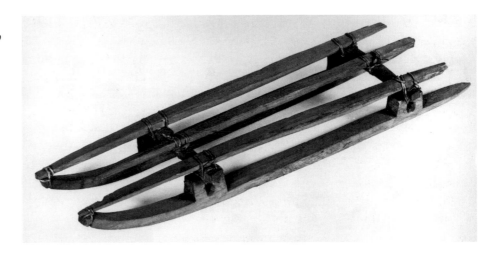

Fig. 25: Toy sled from Ungava Bay, Labrador (photo Smithsonian Institution – Cat No. 89941).

Lucien M. Turner is at the United States National Museum in Washington D.C., and displays similar stanchions (or "jogs" as Otis T. Mason calls them).[71] This sled is 9^1/$_2$ inches long, and as seen in fig 25, has two stanchions on each runner, but otherwise the runners of this sled closely resemble ours. The main difference between the two is that the Ipiutak sled presumably had an arch in place of the forward stanchions.

We shall return to the Labrador sled later, but first we must look into the question of the use of arches as support of the sled's platform. Built-up sleds with arches either instead of posts, or in combination with posts, occur in a limited area, namely among the Chukchee, Noryak, Kamchadal, and Yukaghir of northeastern Asia, and in parts of Alaska – areas that has several other cultural traits in common. According to Bogoras, who has given the most detailed description of sleds in the Asiatic region, arches instead of posts were used with dogs or reindeer, until the middle of the 19th century. Since that time, only reindeer sleds have had arches, while a type of sled with posts was adopted from the south for use with dogs. At the same time, the harness configuration changed from a fan to a tandem pattern.[72]. If Bogoras is right in his statement, it means that (in this area) sleds with arches supporting the platform are older than sleds with posts. The runners on both dog sleds and reindeer sleds are flat, and

generally a little thicker than ours, but have about the same width. The arches were made of antler or wood.

As already mentioned, antler arches were in use in Alaska as early as the Birnirk culture, and through this culture, can be traced as far to the west as Kolyma. We can be fairly certain that the people of northeastern Asia at least as early as Birnirk and probably even earlier used sleds with arches. In Alaska, built-up sleds with arches or some sort of bowed support for the platform have undoubtedly been in use by Eskimos continuously through to the present. There were simple forms like one from Togiak River, illustrated by Mason, with just two arches supporting a platform that consists of one wooden board, but most of the examples from historic time are more elaborate than this. Figure 26 shows a model of a sled type which was widely distributed among the Eskimos of Alaska and which was made for me by an Eskimo from Anaktuvuk Pass. Each of the three arches that are mortised into the runners actually consists of two "knees" spliced together in the middle. Lashed to the arches are two long boards, which support a bed of 9 crossbars and two slats along the sides. Mortised into the runners behind the "knees" are stanchions extending above the bed and supporting a railing. A flat, slightly rounded strip of wood nailed to the runners indicates that they were shoed. Sleds of this type were used in the last century from Barrow and at least as far south as Norton Sound, and Giddings has suggested that a sled with both arches and stanchions has been in general use in

[71] O.T. Mason 1894-96: 572.
[72] Bogoras 1904-09: 99.

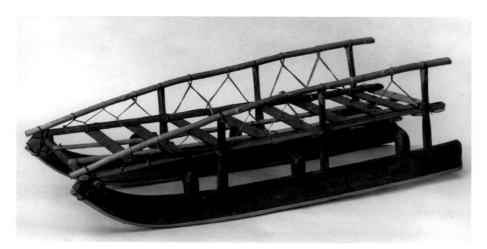

Fig. 26: Model of build-up sled (photo L. Larsen).

Alaska since the 16[73] century. The question is when did it become equipped with a railing? It is possible that this feature is linked with the Chukchees adoption of the Tungus sled, which had stanchions and railings [74]. As mentioned above, this occurred in the 19th century.

Built-up sleds are also known from some of the northern Athapaskans that are neighbors to the Eskimos. The simplest form is used by the Kutchin and is known from the drawings of Murray[75], Jones[76] and from Osgood's description of which I shall quote the following: "The runners are cut in one piece from birch wood and curve up at both ends, making a sledge eight to ten feet long. Three or more birch ribs are bent into a flattened V-shape and these, together with straight horizontal pieces at the ends, join the runners at a width varying from two and one-half to three feet. Lengthwise struts are lashed on top to make a carrying platform. – The sleds are pulled by men or women, and sometimes dogs assist, –"[77]. The sledges formerly used by the Han, illustrated by Osgood[78], are almost identical to the Kutchin sledge. From the sketch it appears that the ribs are shaped like regular arches, which is also the impression one gets from the drawings by Murray and Jones. A model apparently of this type is in

the U.S. National Museum and is said to be from Tanana River, which probably also means that it was used by the Tanana Indians[79]. Their neighbors to the west, the Ingalik, had according to Osgood two types of sleds in the 1930's of which one, the Innoko-type, is a further development of the type described above. It is of the same shape with ends curving up, but furnished with an elevated railing lashed to the ends and held up by posts, as is the case with most later Eskimo sleds from Alaska. The second type only has the front end curved up and is thus more like an Eskimo sled[80].

Of the types of sleds mentioned in the foregoing, the one from Labrador (fig. 25) has the strongest resemblance to the one we are trying to reconstruct. Actually, the only difference is that the former has two pairs of stanchions while the Deering sled probably had an arch instead of the front pair. Because we are left completely in the dark regarding the construction of the bed of our sled, we may take resort to the Labrador sled and the sled from Togiak River, both of which have a simple bed which could have been used on our sled. These beds consist of three slats or boards (and a board in the center), two along the sides lashed to the rear crossbar, a front crossbar or arch, and to the upturned front of the runners. Considering that the Deering sled had an estimated length of 1.50 m, even if it had strongly upturned runner ends, it is likely that for the sake of strength these runners were connected in one or more places, either by another arch or as with the Togiak sled, with a crosspiece. Unfortunately, the material at hand does not allow a better sub-

[73] O.T. Mason 1894-96: fig. 245.
[74] Murdoch 1892: fig. 356; Nelson 1899: Pl. LXXV and LXXVI.16.
[75] Osgood 1936: fig. 8.
[76] Jones 1867: 321.
[77] Osgood 1936: 64.
[78] Osgood 1971: fig. 13.
[79] O.T. Mason 1896: 558.
[80] Osgood 1940: 353-359.

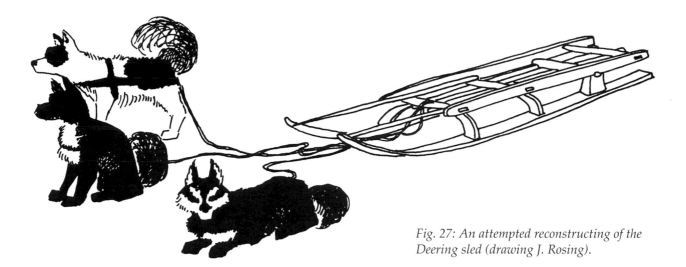

Fig. 27: An attempted reconstructing of the Deering sled (drawing J. Rosing).

stantiated reconstruction of the Ipiutak form of sled than the one presented here (fig. 27). For the time being we must be content with the fact that the Ipiutak people used a rather small and light built-up sled of an unusual type, with flat runners and short, carved out stanchions, connected with a crossbar and one or two wooden arches. We do not know whether man or dogs or both pulled it, but as the find yielded ample evidence of the presence of dogs around the house, I will not exclude the possibility of dog traction. The Labrador sled in fig. 25 is unique and I dare not draw any conclusion regarding a relationship between this and our sled.

Snowshoes

It has often been pointed out that snowshoes are neither an original nor a prominent element in Eskimo culture, but are "more or less successful imitations of the snowshoes of the neighboring Indians".[81] Yet they are known and used by Eskimos from the Bering Strait to Labrador, and it is from excavations of Eskimo sites that we know about snowshoe forms of prehistoric times. In Alaska, in addition to the snowshoe parts to be described here, we have evidence of snowshoe use in the 15th – 18th century from sites on the

Kobuk River,[82] extending back to the 13th century at Nukleet,[83] and from the period of the Western Thule culture at Point Hope[84] and on St. Lawrence Island.[85] The evidence, consisting of parts of frames, crosspieces and snowshoe needles, do not show any significant change from primitive to highly developed forms, but rather that what is known as the Athabascan pointed-toe type has existed in Alaska for many centuries. The best proof of this is the snowshoe parts from Deering to be described in the following.

Twenty wooden pieces in the collection can be identified as parts of snowshoes. Most are in an excellent state of preservation. Unless otherwise noted in the catalogue, they are made of birch wood. Eight of the 20 pieces are parts of frames. Plate 8.9 is an almost complete specimen and only a short piece is missing in what seems to be the front end. The remaining piece is 70 cm long and slightly curved. Most of it is elliptic in cross section, about 2.2 x 1.6 cm but flattening out toward the rear where it is only 0.7 cm thick. There are two pairs of rectangular perforations on the front half and a pair of square holes in the rear section; the space between the holes being approximately 2 cm. In addition, on the inside there are three oblong mortises. One is in front of the first pair of holes, and one behind the second pair, and a third is 6 cm in front of the last pair. Of these mortises, the two first are 2.4 cm long, 0.5 cm wide, and 0.6 cm deep, and the third is only 1.5 cm long and slightly narrower than the other two.

The function of these perforations and mortises is obvious. Lines from the netting have been

81 Birket-Smith 1929(II): 36; Davidson 1937: 4.
82 Giddings 1952: 61-63.
83 Giddings 1964: 82-83.
84 Ipiutak: Pl. 88. 10.
85 Geist and Rainey 1936: 122, 146 & 162.

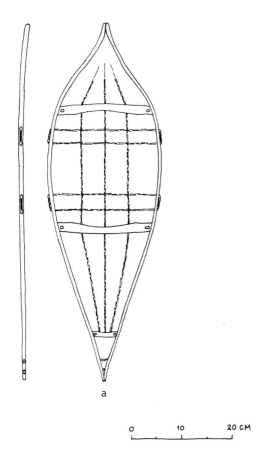
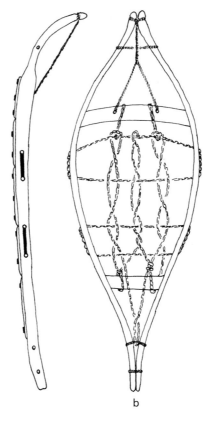

Fig. 28: (a) Reconstructed Deering snowshoe and (b) a King's Island snowshoe, after Davidson 1937 (drawing by H.C. Gulløv).

0   10   20 CM

reeved through the holes in the front part and the two holes in the rear have been used for a lashing to the other frame piece (fig. 28). From the position of the holes and mortises -slightly off the centerline of the frame piece- it seems likely that we are dealing with a left side section. The mortises must be for insertion of crosspieces, which means that there seems to have been two major crosspieces in addition to one minor one in the rear.

Plate 7.1 is a 41.5 cm long piece of a frame which has been made thinner and shorter with coarse cuts. Judging from the arrangement of one oblong mortise and two pairs of perforations for netting, this corresponds to the middle section of the frame piece described above. Plate. 7.2 is a frame fragment with a 2.3 cm long mortise and with a definite, flat underside and a rounded top side.

Plate 7.3 is probably the rear section of a left frame piece, with a 1.2 cm long mortise, a rectangular perforation and a rounded topside and flat underside. There are two more rear sections each with a short mortise. One of them (Pl. 7.4) has two perforations for lashing and a flat underside

showing signs of wear. Each of the remaining two frame pieces has one long mortise. One of these (Pl. 7.6) is elliptical in cross section, and the other is rounded.

There are 10 pieces, which with certainty can be identified as snowshoe crosspieces, one is probably a crosspiece, while another is doubtful. The 10 crosspieces range in length from 16.4 cm (Pl. 7.7) to 23.5 cm (Pl. 7.14) and in width from 1.3 cm (Pl. 7.7) to 2.6 cm (Pl. 7.16). The others measure 1.9 to 2.4 cm at the ends. They are thickest in the middle, up to 2.6 cm (Pl. 7.11), and have wedge-shaped ends to fit into the mortises in the frame. An oblong hole near each end of the crosspieces indicates that they have been secured to the frame by lashing.

Nine of the crosspieces have from two to four oblong, horizontal perforations through the thickest part, while one and possibly a second (Pl. 7.16 and 17) have four vertical perforations. These holes in connection with similar holes in the frame, held the webbing (probably of rawhide lines), that filled the space for the foot. In addition to these perforations, on some of the crosspieces there are one, two, or three small, oblong mortises whose function I am unable to explain. In one case, Pl. 7.9, a short groove for a countersunk line extends from each of two mortises. This seems to me to indicate that these mortises were placed on the topside of the crosspiece.

Of the nine crosspieces with horizontal perforations Pl. 7.7 is of willow. It has two perforations, which on one side are connected with a groove and on the other side a short groove extending to the edge from each of these. Plate 7.9 has two perforations between the two mortises that can be seen on the illustration. Plate. 7.8 and 10 have three perforations, and Pl. 7.11-13 each has three perforations and one, two or three mortises respectively. Plate. 7.14 and 15 have four perforations, and the latter in addition has two mortises.

Plate 7.16 has, in addition to the holes for the lashing to the frame, four oblong, vertical perforations of which the two in the middle are connected with a groove while a short groove extends from each of the other two holes. All undoubtedly were meant for countersunk rawhide lines. Plate 7.17 is also presumably a snowshoe crosspiece, though it is considerably larger than the others (28 x 3-5 cm), is made of spruce, and has a crude, unfinished appearance. As seen in the illustration, it has four oblong, vertical perforations and one end has two holes for lashing. The last and more doubtful piece which may be a crosspiece (elliptical in cross-section) is 12.5 cm long, 2.3 cm wide and has a wedge-shaped end, but without holes.

The material described above shows that Ipiutak snowshoes were anything but primitive. The uniformity in size and shape of the crosspieces and the great care that has been bestowed on their manufacture, tell us that snowshoes have been an element in the Ipiutak culture for a long time. It also tells us that the Ipiutak type of snowshoe is surprisingly similar to snowshoes used in the same area in historical times and which Davidson designates as Athabascan. Using his classification we can say that the Ipiutak people had a two-piece frame snowshoe. This probably had a pointed toe (not upturned nor with a pointed

heel), two or three crosspieces, netting confined to the foot space and made with the use of the reeving method of attachment. Most likely the netting was a rectangular weave. An attempt to make a reconstruction of the Ipiutak snowshoe based on the material from Deering is shown in fig. 28.

Comparing the Ipiutak snowshoes with later forms, we find the closest resemblance to snowshoes from King Island, St. Lawrence Island, and the Chukchee.[86] The only significant difference is that the longitudinal strands of the netting are wrapped around the crosspieces and not reeved through them, a feature characteristic of the Ipiutak snowshoe. Another difference is the turned-up toe as it occurs, for instance, on the King Island snowshoe. This is a late trait according to Davidson, who says that "there seems no reason for doubting that the earliest types of snowshoes were flat and that the turned-up toe was a later development".[87]

The reeving method of attachment to the frame and the rectangular weave of the netting for the foot rest are traits the Ipiutak snowshoe has in common with most other snowshoes in Alaska. The two traits have similar distribution; namely an area covering the northeastern most regions of Siberia, Alaska, and the Mackenzie district. While the reeving technique is limited to this area, the rectangular weave occurs sporadically elsewhere in North America.[88] The center of distribution is in Alaska, and there can be no doubt that the occurrence of snowshoes with these two traits in northeastern Siberia is due to influence from Alaska. The Deering find shows that this could have occurred as early as AD 600 if not earlier.

In Alaska outside the Bering Strait region, the snowshoes of both Eskimos and Indians have developed into much more elaborate forms. Most conspicuous is the filling of the toe and the heel compartments with a fine, hexagonal weave of babiche or twisted sinew. According to Davidson, "hexagonal weaving represents a much more complex development, and this coupled with the distributional factors would seem definitely to indicate a more recent application to snowshoes."[89] The question is how recent, as there are strong indications that Eskimo snowshoes were furnished with at least some form of a fine-meshed filling several hundred years ago. In the first place, as Giddings has pointed out, referring

---

[86] Davidson 1937: figs. 32 and 33.
[87] Davidson 1937: 110.
[88] Davidson 1937: figs. 12 and 13.
[89] Davidson 1937: 35.

Fig. 29: Toy canoe-like vessel with carved figure in the middle, from the Qalegi. *The vessel is 21.4 cm long (photo L. Larsen).*

to snowshoe parts from the earliest Nukleet times "Eskimo coastal people made fine snowshoes as much as seven hundred years ago".[90] Furthermore, the presence of snowshoe needles as far back as the time of the Western Thule culture[91] must mean that snowshoes then must have been furnished with fine-meshed netting of thin strands, probably in the toe or heel compartments or both, as the coarse, rectangular netting in the foot-section was undoubtedly made without the use of a needle.

Another feature that is characteristic of later Alaskan snowshoes is the rounded, spliced toe which occurs concurrently with the pointed toe and which Davidson considers to be a recent acquisition.[92] A good example of both types is illustrated by Giddings in his publication "The Arctic Woodland Culture of the Kobuk River." This shows that the middle part of the modern Alaska Eskimo snowshoe with its foot-rest of a coarse, rectangular netting reeved through the frame, has remained unchanged since Ipiutak times.[93]

Boats

Though the Ipiutak material excavated at Point Hope did not contain any remains of boats nor boat accessories, we took it for granted that when the Ipiutak people were equipped for hunting

aquatic animals they must also have had boats, and we even went so far as to say that we assumed that they had umiaks as well as kayaks.[94] This assumption seems to be premature. Although we did find definite proof of the use of boats, we have only uncertain evidence of the use of umiaks, and the model of a boat we did find is not that of a true kayak (fig. 29). The little boat shown here is made of poplar bark and is 21.4 cm long, 2.3 cm wide, and 2.3 cm high. The crudely carved figure in the middle of the boat is 3.4 cm high and has a pointed base which is inserted in a hole in a low pedestal extending from the bottom. The largest part of the boat has been hollowed out to a depth of about 1 cm leaving a gunwale 0.6 cm wide and a "decked" bow and stern, respectively 5 and 2.9 cm long. The "bow-deck" is slightly curved from side to side and is slanting toward the bow which seems to have been pointed and upturned but is broken off. The boat and figure show remains of red paint, probably hematite.

Whether this boat is a toy or has served some other purpose, we can be fairly certain that the Ipiutak people at that time possessed a type of boat with the essential features similar to this. According to definition a kayak must be completely decked except for (usually) one manhole[95] and our boat for the most part was undecked, so I prefer to call it a canoe. Partly decked birch bark canoes were formerly used as hunting canoes by practically all the northern Athapaskans from Chipewyans in the east to the Ingalik and the Tanaina in the west.[96] They were flat-bottomed with pointed ends and were decked fore and aft or at least in front. One man placed in the middle of the boat, usually kneeling, propelled them. In their book on "The Bark Canoes and Skin Boats of North America" Adney and Chapelle describe

[90] Giddings 1964: 82-83.
[91] Ipiutak: Pl. 88.10.
[92] Davidson 1937: 135.
[93] Giddings 1952: fig. 33.
[94] Ipiutak: 77.
[95] Arima 1963: 38.
[96] Larsen 1982.

them as kayak-form canoes and characterize them as highly developed in both model and construction.[97] They range in length from 12 to 18 feet, are 24-27 inches wide and between 9 and 12 inches deep. On the canoes from the upper Yukon, the bow deck was about one fifth the length of the boat, on the lower Yukon nearly one third. Though primarily known from the Athapaskans, the birch bark canoe of the kayak-form was also used by some of the Alaska Eskimos. Of Adney's and Chapelle's drawings of canoes of this type, one is stated to be an Eskimo canoe from the Alaska coast another from the lower Yukon.[98] It is possible, however, that at least the lower Yukon one was made by Ingalik Indians, as bark canoes were one of the items the Eskimos acquired through trade with the Indians.[99]

Birch bark canoes with decked bows were not only used, but also made by Eskimos not far from Deering, namely the Kobuk River Eskimos. Naval lieutenant John C. Cantwell, who explored the Kobuk in 1884, describes "lighter canoes of exquisite design... made of birch bark stretched over frames of well-seasoned wood", which were used exclusively by hunters. They were eight to ten feet long by two feet wide at the "greatest breadth of beam, a little forward of the center.... From here the sides curve to a point at each end. They are undecked except for a short distance forward, where a piece of bark ... across the bow is secured by lashings of willow bark". These canoes are frail, and weigh no more than twenty-five pounds.[100] When Giddings worked in the Kobuk area in the 1940s the birch bark canoes had been replaced by what he called river "kayaks". They were covered with canvas but with a frame that is identical to that of the bark canoe.[101] The same change from bark to canvas has taken place with some of the Athapaskan canoes of this type.[102] One of Giddings' informants could add the infor-

mation that the birch bark canoes were decked for one-quarter to one-third of its length from the bow, that they had a forward extension of the prow, and that the less desirable spruce bark was substituted for birch bark when the latter was not accessible.[103] Another informant gave a detailed description of the materials used, the collecting of the materials, and the whole process of building a birch bark canoe.[104]

The conformity of the kayak-form bark canoe of the Athapaskans and the Kobuk Eskimos with regard to materials, construction, and shape leaves no doubt about their common origin. The most likely place of origin must be an area where suitable materials, particularly bark, are available in sufficient quantities; hence we must conclude that it originated in the boreal forest, the habitat of most northern Athapaskans. It would thus seem that the Athapaskans rather than the Eskimos, who habitually live outside the forest, are the inventors of this type of boat. Before making a statement to that effect we must not forget that birch bark canoes are not limited to America but occur also in eastern Siberia. In his work on the peoples of the Amur region, Leopold von Schrenck illustrates a birch bark canoe from the Oltscha (Ul'chi) at the mouth of the Amur River, which shows points of similarities with the kayak-form canoe.[105] The most conspicuous similarity is that it is decked fore and aft. It has pointed ends, although the points are below the water, like on the bark canoes of the Interior Salish.[106] The dimensions are about the same as the hunting canoes of the Athapaskans. Other peoples used the same type of bark canoe as for instance, the Goldi and the Evenk.[107] The canoes of the latter had pointed ends that were level with the gunwale.

Returning to our boat model, one may ask if it is a model of a bark canoe of the type described above, in which case we must assume that the Ipiutak people at Deering used bark canoes. Off hand this does not seem very likely, considering that Deering is far away from any source of birch and spruce bark. The closest is probably on the Kobuk River about which Giddings writes that "large birch trees of the sort needed for stripping bark for boats and utensils are scarce below Ahteut."[108] This means that the Deering people had to travel about 150 miles as the crow flies to

---

[97] Adney & Chapelle 1964: 158-168.
[98] Adney & Chapelle 1964: fig. 147 and fig. 150.
[99] de Laguna 1947: 33.
[100] Cantwell 1889: 84
[101] Giddings 1952: 59 and fig. 34; Giddings 1961: 146.
[102] McKennan 1959: 93.
[103] Giddings 1961: 146.
[104] Giddings 1961: 36-39.
[105] von Schrenck 1881: Pl. XXXVIII and fig. 5.
[106] Jenness 1932: 107.
[107] Levin and Potapov 1964: 634 and 704.
[108] Giddings 1952: 86.

obtain birch bark usable for boat covering. That they did acquire bark in considerable quantities is, however, evident from the masses of pieces of birch bark that were lying in and around the Ipiutak house. We discarded most of the pieces but saved a considerable number with holes from sewing or other signs of having been worked. None were large enough to suggest parts of boat covering. For this and other reasons to be discussed below, I am inclined to believe that the Ipiutak boat was covered with skin rather than birch bark.

The strongest indication of skin covering is the presence in the refuse outside the house of two pieces of sealskin that very well could be parts of boat covers. The largest piece, Pl. 8.7, has a waterproof seam running almost its entire length and in addition there are three small holes that have been carefully mended, undoubtedly with the intention of making the skin watertight. Creases on the other pieces indicate that they are part of the same piece, which makes it even more likely that we are dealing with a boat cover. Judging by the thickness of the skin we must assume that it belonged to a small boat, rather than an umiak. A boat model reminiscent of ours has been found with other boat models of bark at the Birnirk site. Some have a flat deck and a hole in the middle for a figure undoubtedly representing kayaks, while the larger ones without deck must be umiak models. The one in question, "has an upturned bow like the kayak models and the lines of a kayak, but it is hollowed out like an Indian dugout canoe. A raised area in the bottom, with a small hole for inserting the figure of a single man, shows that this is intended to represent a small, one-man boat, not an umiak".[109] Except for the missing deck fore and aft, it is very much like our model from Deering; in particular the raised area in the bottom with a hole for a figure is worth noting. Excluding the possibility of a dugout, we must assume that it is the model of a boat similar to those used in Ipiutak-times at Deering. Considering the distance from Barrow to any source of bark, we may take it for granted that it was cov-

ered with skin and it thus supports our assumption that the Ipiutak craft was skin covered.

Of the three types of boats used at Barrow in Birnirk times, the canoe was probably primarily used in inland waters while the kayak and the umiak could be used in the open sea as well. Models of kayaks and umiaks similar to those from Birnirk occur in Old Bering Sea finds on St. Lawrence Island. Considering that whaling and sealing with floats were practiced at the Okvik stage, it seems likely that both types of boats were also used at that stage.[110] In the Ipiutak culture we can only be certain of the use of one of the types, the kayak-formed canoe, that I believe is related to the Birnirk canoe. Unless Pl. 8.3 is part of an umiak oar, a possibility that must be considered, there is in the finds from Deering no definite evidence of the use of any of the other two types of boats. Based on some similarity with kayak bow pieces from Birnirk,[111] the three wooden pieces illustrated in Pl. 8.4-6 have tentatively been identified as bow pieces; actually, our model originally had some sort of a protruding prow.

From the foregoing we may conclude that the Ipiutak people used a partly decked boat of the same or similar type as the kayak-formed birch bark canoe known by practically all northern Athapaskans and some Alaskan Eskimos. That the Ipiutak boat probably was covered with skin rather then bark is a difference of minor significance when we know about the Chipewyan "that when they were in Barren Grounds in summer and lacked birch bark, they covered their canoes with caribou skin".[112]

The presence of a partly decked boat in the Ipiutak culture raises the old question of the origin of the kayak. Gudmud Hatt brings it up already in 1916 in an article on coast and inland-cultures in the Arctic, which appeared in the Danish geographical journal, "Geografisk Tidsskrift". Although Hatt realizes that the use of skin boats in itself is older than the use of sewn bark boats, he states that it is a not uncommon assumption that the birch bark canoe is the prototype from which the Eskimo kayak has developed. Because his article is written in Danish, I shall quote in translation his arguments in favor of the theory: "What particularly supports the theory about the development of the kayaks from the birch bark canoe is the circumstance that in Siberia as well as

[109] Ford 1959: 157 and fig. 78 d.
[110] Collins 1937: Pl. 59.1 and 6.
[111] Ford 1959: 79.a-b.
[112] Birket-Smith 1929: 172.
[113] Hatt 1916: 287-288.

in North America there are birch bark canoes that are partly covered. Furthermore some tribes in the Central Eskimo area use the kayak to hunt swimming caribou when crossing rivers on their yearly migration in the same way as inland hunters in Siberia and North America hunt wild reindeer from canoe."[113] Birket-Smith disagrees with Hatt's view on the origin of the kayak. He does not find Hatt's arguments convincing, and sticks to his formerly expressed opinion that "the kayak and the compound bark canoe, must rather be looked upon as specializations, each in its own direction from a mutual fundamental form, a primitive skin boat."[114] I agree with Birket-Smith that the fundamental form must be a simple open skin boat, but I do not think it is unreasonable to assume that a partly decked skin boat led to the invention of the fully decked kayak.

Paddles

Of the three paddle-shaped objects illustrated in Pl. 8, only Pl. 8.1 is definitely the blade of a paddle. It is made of spruce, 43 cm long and 10.3 cm wide. The shaft is 3.3 cm in diameter. The surface shows traces of fire, probably from the process of shaping it, as is known from Ingalik.[115] Despite their present appearance the other two paddle-shaped objects have undoubtedly been made for the same purpose. They are made of coarse-grained spruce and have a flat or slightly concave side while the other side is slightly convex. The shafts, 3.4 cm in diameter, form a low keel on the uppermost part of the reverse side. Both show faint traces of black paint (?), Pl. 8.3 also of red paint at base of the shaft. Plate 8.2 has obviously been made much smaller by cuts along both edges, the larger specimen is split along an annual ring. If it originally were symmetrical, it would have been 40 cm long and 35 cm wide. The interpretation of these two pieces is uncertain, on one hand they could have been used as boat paddles, on the other hand the shaft does not seem sturdy

enough for such a large blade. Another possibility is that they are shovel blades.

TOOLS

Wooden knife handles

With 26 more or less complete wooden knife handles, the Deering find fully confirms the presumption expressed in the Ipiutak report that "wooden handles were extensively used" and "that knives with wooden handle and side blade were common" in the Ipiutak culture. [116] The presumption was based on the fact that, though only three wooden handles were found, the Ipiutak find from Point Hope contains 367 bifacially chipped flint blades, which were classified as knife side blades. In the Deering find there are only 14 side blades of which six were found in their handles. These are all of spruce and for the most part carefully made. According to the number and placing of the side blades, the knife handles may be divided into three types, one for a single side blade, one for two side blades, and one for an end-side blade.

Wooden knife handles for a single side blade
Of the wooden handles, 20 belong to this group, to which also belongs the three from Point Hope.[117] A selection of the best preserved is illustrated in Plate 9 which shows the variation in shape and size. Pl. 9.1, which is 22.2 cm long, is the largest and the best preserved. The groove for the blade is 6.5 cm long, 0.6 cm wide and 1.5 cm deep. The back of the handle is decorated with three, short, transversal and parallel incised lines back of the blade and a similar line on the back of the grip. The blade, made of black silicified slate, was found in situ as shown in Pl. 9.1. As with the other side blades found at Deering, the execution of the blade as far as chipping technique is concerned is the same as described for the side blades from Point Hope Ipiutak. [118] Of the seven types of side blades from Point Hope, the blade in question shows the closest resemblance to Type 6. The blades of this type are characterized as: "mostly broad, with flat, slanting base", and of the specimens illustrated in the Ipiutak report (Pl. 13.12-16) our blade shows considerable similarity to Figs. 12

---

[114] Birket-Smith 1929: 172.
[115] Osgood 1940: 373-374.
[116] Ipiutak: 81.
[117] Ipiutak: figs. 16, 17, and 21.
[118] Ipiutak: 99.

and 15. It is interesting to notice, however, that what in the Ipiutak report has been described, as the base actually seems to be the top.

Four more handles from Deering resemble Pl. 9.1 in having a definite grip terminating in a more or less pronounced knob, that is Pl. 9.2, 6, and 7 and a smaller one not illustrated. The rather straight bottom of the blade groove distinguishes Pl. 9.2. On the reverse side is a narrow groove for a lashing like Pl. 9.1. Pl. 9.6 has the same kind of short, parallel, transversal lines on the back of the handle. Two other features are worth noticing, the unusually long (8 cm) blade groove and the indentations on the grip for the fingers. We find exactly the same indentations for the fingers even with the same oblique lines and the grip illustrated in Pl. 9.7. This specimen is the best preserved piece of wood in the collection and is unusual in other respects. It is made of compression-wood which is formed in branches that have been exposed to long pressure; it is red-brown, horny, has an abnormally high specific gravity, and breaks relatively easily. This piece has a very smooth surface either from wear or intentional polishing. The fourth, small specimen is broken off above the grip.

Plate 9.3 is unique on account of its size, being only 13.9 cm long. The blade, which is so firmly imbedded in the groove that it cannot be removed, is of brown jasper and 4.8 cm long. Three short, parallel, transverse lines are discernible on the back of the handle.

Plate 9.11 and 12 are two handles out of four that have a grip of somewhat uniform shape, a thickening that probably has served to give a better hold. Pl. 9.12 also has an indentation for a finger on the blade side. One has a defect blade-part, the others have blade grooves ranging from 7 to 8 cm in length and from 0.4 to 0.6 cm in width. Pl. 9.4 is distinguished by its characteristic grip and a more than 9 cm long groove for a blade (to the left in the illustration). The grip shows traces of the implements used in the manufacture of the handle, namely beaver tooth knife and stone scraper. Pl. 9.5 with a somewhat similar grip has a 6.4 cm long blade-groove in the edge to the left and a 5.3 cm long groove in the opposite side. The reason why it has not been classed as a handle with two side blades is due to the shape of the grip, which makes me believe that the right groove is sec-

ondary, and was made when the other one broke. The collection also contains a fragment of a grip similar to the above.

Two more handles (Pl. 9.8 and 10) were found with the blade in place. Pl. 9.8 is rather simple, not much more than a flat wooden stick with a 7 cm long groove in one edge. The blade of gray flint has been broken lengthwise; hence it cannot be classified. It is possible that Pl. 9.10 should be classified as a special type because below the groove with the blade, there is part of another groove which means that the handle might have held two side blades. As this is the only case of a knife handle with two side blades in continuation of each other the explanation might be that the grooves did not hold blades at the same time. The blade found in situ is symmetrical, with a clear distinction between the finely chipped cutting edge and the coarse chipping of the part that has been wedged into the handle. It is typical of the Point Hope Ipiutak side blades Type 1 and practically identical with the one illustrated in Pl. 12.3.

Of the six more or less fragmentary handles which make up the total of this group, Pl. 9.9 is the largest and best preserved. Only the top part is missing. It is elliptical in cross-section and is reminiscent of a wooden knife handle for a side blade from the Uwelen-Okvik site in Siberia illustrated by S.I.Rudenko (Pl. 4.1). Of the other five specimens, two (18 cm long) are almost complete, one is a middle section, and two are blade parts with grooves 6.5 and 3.7 cm long respectively.

Wooden knife handles for two side blades

Four rather uniform wooden handles constitute a type characterized by having two opposite blade grooves near the end (Pl. 10. 1-3). As already mentioned Pl. 9.5 may also belong to this group. Pl. 10.1 is extremely well preserved. On the lower part, the marks of the beaver tooth knife used in the manufacture are clearly visible, while the upper part shows sign of wear. The two side blades, which are 6.1 and 5.2 cm long respectively, are so firmly wedged into their grooves that they cannot be removed without damaging the handle; hence they cannot be classified. Meanwhile, it is worth noting that they are different in shape as well as in size. Pl. 10.2 is also well preserved, showing marks of a beaver tooth knife as well as stone scrapers. The blade grooves are 6.7 and 5.7

cm long respectively. One specimen not illustrated is very similar to Pl. 10.2 having the same form of grip. It is 17.2 cm long, 2.7 cm wide, and has 5.1 cm long blade grooves. Pl. 10.3 is quite simple in shape and has blade grooves 4.9 and 4.7 cm long.

This type of knife handle has to my knowledge not been found before, although it is very likely that the Ipiutak people at Point Hope also used it. Not a single *ulu* handle has been found in the Ipiutak sites at Point Hope or Deering, but as numerous side blades with a curved edge were found at Ipiutak and the knife handles described above at Deering, there can be no doubt that this kind of knife, with one or two side blades, has had at least some of the same functions as the *ulu*. In my opinion, they are flenshing knives used primarily for skinning animals and for cutting up meat.

According to Rudenko, no *ulus* but numerous knives for side blades were found at Uwelen, and even if a few short ivory handles may be classified as *ulu* handles we must assume that the majority are knives with side blades of slate and flint.[119] The Okvik site on Punuk Islands contained typical *ulus* as well as knives with side blades, although the grip part in some cases is so short that it seems to be of little use. The blades are of ground or chipped slate.[120]

Wooden knife handles for end-side blade

Pl. 10.4 deviates from the knife handles described above in that it has a rather short blade groove that is open in the end, which means that the blade must have extended beyond the handle. The groove is 3.5 cm long and 0.5 cm wide. The blade has been secured by a lashing that has left faint traces on the surface. The handle, which is 1.9 cm thick, has a sturdy appearance and the indentations for the fingers add to the impression that it was made for heavy work. Meanwhile, the absence in the find of any kind of blade that would fit the socket leaves us without a suggestion regarding the function of this unique form of knife handle.

Knife handles for end blades

Three knife handles of antler (Pl. 11.1-3) have a socket for a blade in the end, but otherwise they have little in common. The Ipiutak find from Point Hope also contained three knife handles of antler with blade socket in the end and were classified as knife handles of type 2.[121] Pl. 11.1 is unique on account of the ornamentation, which there is reason to believe originally covered the entire surface; the reverse side is now missing. The socket is 1.4 cm long, 0.5 cm wide, and 1.6 cm deep and has probably held a stone blade. This is presumably also true of the handle illustrated in Pl. 11.2, which has a socket of the same width and 2.1 cm deep. The end is damaged by chewing, probably by dogs, but there are still remnants of a ridge which has supported a lashing. In the butt end is a coarsely cut, oblong hole for a suspension strap and on the opposite side a 4 cm long, 1 cm deep, and 0.5 cm wide groove open in the end. In this respect, it is reminiscent of a knife handle illustrated in the Ipiutak report Pl. 8.4. The third handle, Pl. 11.3, has a blade socket or rather a groove, which is only 1 mm wide and 7 mm deep and could only hold a metal blade, probably of iron. The handle is very carefully made and is decorated with a longitudinal groove terminating in an oblong suspension hole.

Handles for splitting knives

The handles described under this heading are the same as the Point Hope handles classified as knife handles, type 3. The term "splitting and engraving knives" was first applied by Birket-Smith[122] and I prefer it because it cover its function better than any of the other terms applied to this tool, "antler chisel", "whittling knife", "composite or compound knife handle". Actually it was Mathiassen, though using the term "whittling knife", who gave the first description of its use and its Eskimo name, "*quingusaq*". "The *quingusaq*", writes Mathiassen, "is principally used for cutting out grooves in bone, for instance when a piece of antler or ivory is to be split. The knife is then gripped with the whole hand, the blade turned downward and it is repeatedly drawn towards the body with great force until the piece is split".[123] The knife to which Mathiassen referred to was from the Iglulik Eskimos and had an iron blade, but already Knud Rasmussen realized that the *quingusaq* was a

[119] Rudenko 1961: 33-34 and Pl. 3.17-27.
[120] Rainey 1941: figs. 18-19.
[121] Ipiutak: Pl. 8.9.
[122] Birket-Smith 1945: fig. 174.
[123] Mathiassen 1928: 104.

"common Palaeolithic implement that has also been used in Denmark, where flint took the place of iron".[124] He could not know that at one time the Eskimos also used a flint blade in this kind of implement. Iron began to replace flint already in the Okvik stage of the Eskimo culture.[125]

At Deering, as at Point Hope, handles for splitting knives constitute the most common form of knife handles. The Deering find contains 26 specimens, 20 of antler and 6 of walrus ivory. Seven are complete and there are no parts of composite handles. In comparison, there were 33 specimens at Point Hope, 19 of antler and 14 of ivory, 3 were complete and 3 halves of the composite type. The Deering specimens form a rather uniform type ranging in length from 11.1 to 8.5 cm. The complete specimens (Pl. 11.4-8) are about 2 cm wide and from 1.0 to 1.3 cm thick, but some of the others, particularly those of ivory, are thicker. The simplest forms consist of a flat piece of the outer layer of antler without any surface treatment (Pl. 11.4), but most of them, and especially the ivory specimens, have a smooth surface and even decoration. All of them are split through the middle of the flat side about two thirds of the length, they have a 5.8 mm long, 5-18 mm deep and 1-2 mm socket for a metal blade in one end, and below it a ridge as support for a lashing.

With one exception all the complete specimens are rather crude. The only trace of surface treatment is in thinning the butt end, as seen in Pl. 11.5 and 6. The exception (Pl. 11.8) is elliptical in cross section and the lower half is decorated with thin, parallel lines. A knife handle from Point Hope has a suspension hole and similar decoration.[126] A simple line decoration is also found on two of the six ivory handles (Pl. 11.9 and 15) which all have a smooth, rounded surface. Three handles of antler have some sort of decoration; Pl. 11.13 a sketchy nondescript figure, and Pl. 11.14 and 16 a deeply cut line, which also occurs on at least one knife handle from point Hope Ipiutak. Of the

other illustrated specimens, Pl. 11.10 has a deeply cut groove at the base of the longitudinal cut, undoubtedly made for lashing applied after a breakage. Pl. 11.11 are hollowed out in the butt, possibly for insertion of a stone blade, as on a handle from Point Hope.[127] The butt of Pl. 11.12 has been sharpened to a point and used as an awl. While the splitting knives in the Old Bering Sea, Punuk, Birnirk, and Thule cultures always consist of two pieces (composite handles) the one-piece form appears in later culture stages in North Alaska as pointed out by Ford.[128] In a collection from Point Barrow purchased by the 5th Thule Expedition is a specimen like the one described and illustrated by Ford. It is 15.2 cm long and 2.2 cm wide, and has a 1.5 cm long, 1.5 cm deep, and 1 mm wide blade groove. Except for its size it is exactly like the handles described above. To explain the disappearance and reappearance of this type, Ford offers the suggestion that "it must have been retained through the intervening time in some neighbouring area".

Beaver Tooth Knives

Six beaver incisors, four of them with traces of wear, and the fact that several wooden specimens show sign of having been worked with a beaver tooth knife provide clear evidence for the use of this implement by the Deering Ipiutak people. Three of the teeth are like Pl. 11.17, lower incisors ranging in length from 6.3 to 6.9 cm, the rest are fragmentary. One of the latter is of particular interest because it has been heavily ground on three sides making it into a chisel-like instrument.

No handles were found and it is possible that they were used unhafted as was one type of beaver tooth tool from the Ingalik.[129] On the other hand they may have been hafted as were the "beaver tooth wood chisel" or the beaver tooth "drawknife" of the Ingalik.[130] We can also refer to examples of hafted beaver teeth from the Eskimos. In the Nukleet site at Cape Denbigh, Giddings found a number of beaver teeth and handles, both for end-hafting and side-hafting, corresponding to those described by Osgood from the Ingalik.[131] Beaver teeth and handles were also found in some of the Kobuk sites, for example in Intermediate Kotzebue[132], and beaver tooth tools were still in use in Alaska when E.W. Nelson made his collections between 1877 and 1881. He mentions that

---

[124] Rasmussen 1932: 101.
[125] Rainey 1941: fig. 18.
[126] Ipiutak: Pl. 8.11.
[127] Ipiutak: Pl. 8.13.
[128] Ford 1959: 165-166 and fig. 81g.
[129] Osgood 1940: 84.
[130] Osgood 1940: 85-88.
[131] Giddings 1964: 55 and 58.
[132] Giddings 1952: Pl. XXXIX.15-16.

they were "used as a gouge for making the hollows for the fingers in throwing-sticks, for cutting grooves, and for excavating hollows in fashioning boxes, masks, spoons, and wooden dishes. The smooth back of the tooth is also used as a polishing instrument for finishing woodwork, and the carved outer edge serves for sharpening knives by rubbing it sharply along the blades".[133] It thus seems that beaver tooth tools have been used by Eskimos wherever beaver teeth are available.

One rodent incisor considerably smaller than beaver teeth, being only 0.5 mm wide, proved to be of porcupine and it has presumably been used in the same way as beaver incisors. In this connection I wish to call attention to the wooden handle, Pl. 10.4, which I described as a knife handle for end-side blade, but which actually may be a handle for a tool corresponding to the beaver tooth knives but used with an incisor smaller than beaver incisors. The suggestion is based on the similarity of this handle with some of those mentioned from Nukleet and Intermediate Kotzebue.

Flake Tools

Pl. 11.18 and 19 are two specimens of the same kind of implement found in the 5th layer of the house. They consist of a wooden stick partly split from one end and with a raw flint flake inserted in the split. Pl. 11.18 has a shaft elliptical in cross section and with a smooth surface. The flake is of grey flint and has a finely retouched lower edge, which may be the result of wear. The shaft of the other specimen is square in cross section; it is broken off at both ends and has the same kind of fine retouch along the lower edge as Pl. 11.18. The flake is held in place by a lashing of willow or spruce root.

Despite the retouch on the edge of both flakes, I doubt that they served a practical purpose and I suggest they are toys, however there are implements that are very similar in shape and which I believe have been used as tools. They were found in 1932 in the opposite end of the Eskimo territory, namely in Northeast Greenland. Five specimens

of an implement consisting of a raw flake inserted in a wooden shaft were found in the first stage of the mixed culture in Dødemandsbugten and interpreted as baleen cutters.[134] The interpretation was based on the fact that all the flakes ended in a sharp point and that experiments had shown that they actually could be used in cutting up baleen into thin strips. Another similar implement, described as a stone bone cutter, is known from the Ingalik and used as burins for cutting grooves in bone.[135] In both cases the similarity seems to be incidental; at least our specimens could not be used for either purpose. On the other hand, if they are toys they must imitate some tool used by the adults, but I am unable to make any suggestions as to the nature of this.

Engraving Tools

Only one half of an engraving tool was found at Deering (Pl. 13.10). It is the upper half of one made of ivory, with a decoration consisting of 8 knobs arranged in two horizontal rows around the middle of the implement. It is unpolished and the surface shows marks of a stone-scraper. Like most of the engraving tools from Ipiutak, it has a conical butt (or top) which shows sign of wear caused by rotation. Regarding the spatial and temporal distribution of engraving tools, I can refer to the Ipiutak report.[136]

Adzes

The find contains a number of parts of adzes. These adzes consist of antler heads with a deep socket for a stone blade and wooden handles, in general not unlike those from the Ipiutak site at Point Hope. As at Point Hope, adze heads of type 1 are the most common (with 17 specimens). They vary in length from 13.6 cm (Pl. 12.7) to 6.4 cm (Pl. 12.10); in both cases without the blade. In width, they range from 2.7 cm (Pl. 12.2) to 5.3 cm. The range of variation in shape is shown in Pl. 12. 1-10. There is considerable variation in the execution, some like Pl. 12.1 and 10 are very well made, but the majority are simply a piece of antler hollowed out in one end for a blade and with a more or less pronounced groove for a lashing. Pl. 12.5

---

[133] Nelson 1899: 89, fig. 25 and Pl. XXXVIII.21 and 23.
[134] Larsen 1934: 118, fig. 29 and Pl. 5.6.
[135] Osgood 1940: 94.
[136] Ipiutak: 82-84.

Fig. 30: Shovel blade from Qalegi. The blade is 41 cm long (photo L. Larsen).

Shovels

Whalebone shovels, quite common at Point Hope, are represented here by one large and one small, dubious specimen. Like the whalebone shovels from Point Hope the large fragment is a 35 cm long and 13.2 cm wide piece of a whale rib, sharpened along the edge and cut off in the rear end. Except for a lack of holes near the edge and that it is more rounded in the end, it is reminiscent of the whalebone shovel described in the Ipiutak Report (Pl. 21.2). The other shovels from Deering are of spruce.

Figure 30 is a large shovel blade with an incision for a shaft. It is impossible to see how the shaft was fastened. The blade is 41 cm long, 34 cm wide and from 2.2 to 1.2 cm thick. The under side is slightly convex. This as well as the other wooden shovels may have been used as snow shovels but may also have served other purposes. A wooden snow shovel with a wide blade and a long shaft from Point Barrow is illustrated by E.W. Nelson (Pl. XXXV.4). In addition to fig. 30 the find contains half a blade of similar shape and 44 cm long. In connection with the description of oars, it was mentioned that Pl. 8.2 and 3 might be oars but that I was more inclined to interpret them as parts of shovels. They are made of the same kind of wood as the two shovel blades described above, they are slightly concave on one side and slightly convex on the other, and the shaft extends to the convex side. As already mentioned, one must assume that Pl. 8.3 originally was symmetrical in relation to the shaft and that Pl. 8.2 has been reduced considerably in size. It deserves mentioning that both specimens show traces of black paint, the larger one also of red.

Fish Scalers

In the Ipiutak Report is illustrated (Pl. 29.16) an "implement with sharp, curved edge, made of caribou scapula" but with no explanation as to it's use. Since then, similar implements have been found and described by Giddings in sites on the Kobuk River and at Cape Denbigh, so that we now know that it was not an isolated case but that it belongs to a not uncommon type of implement within the Eskimo culture. In his description of the finds from Kobuk, Giddings names it a scaler of caribou scapula and says that it is "an inland trait that runs through 11 periods" and that "Eskimos who have used the tool insist that it had no other purpose than that of scaling fish".[140] Later, in describing the Nukleet find where the "scapula scrapers" occur in all levels, he is inclined to consider them as "multi-purpose tools".[141] In the Deering find there are four of these scapula scrapers, three of them found in the same layer of the house. They are made of caribou scapula and range in length from 15.5 to 10.8 cm (Pl. 13.13 and 14) and have a sharp, longitudinal edge. In mentioning these scrapers as an inland trait Giddings is referring to Frederica de Laguna who has demonstrated their wide distribution in time and space.[142]

Two-handed scrapers

Another type of bone scraper, the so-called two-handed scraper or beaming tool, has been dealt with extensively in the Ipiutak report, so suffice to say that three fragmentary specimens were found at Deering.[143] Two of the specimens were the distal ends of caribou metatarsals (like Pl. 13.11) and the third the proximal end of the same (Pl. 13.12).

[140] Giddings 1952: 40.
[141] Giddings 1964: 69-70.
[142] de Laguna 1947: 191.
[143] Ipiutak: 88-90.

Needles

Seven bone needles were found, three of them complete with a tiny round eye in one end (Pl. 18.1-3). Pl. 18.2 is 2 mm thick and was originally longer; it was broken above the present eye and a new eye made. The other two complete specimens are only 1 mm thick and have of course a still smaller eye. They can only have been used for very fine needlework. The seven needles were all found in the 5th layer of the house. In and around the house were found 23 bird bones that have been used in making the needles (Pl. 18.4-9). With three exceptions, the bones used are humeri of goose, the exceptions being two humeri of swan (Pl. 18.7) and one goose ulna (Pl. 18.8). The maker probably used a splitting knife with a thin blade to cut thin slivers out of the bone and then ground the slivers down to the suitable size. The perfectly round eye must have been drilled, probably from two sides, but the drill bit used in the process is an open question.

Awls

87 specimens have been classified as awls (Pl. 18.10-16), most of them antler, 15 of ivory and one of bone. There is a great variation in shape and they range in size from 15.8 to 3.5 cm. A considerable number are made from weapon heads, particularly arrowheads, and probably none of them were originally intended to be used as awls. The many awls in the find is undoubtedly due to the extensive use of birch bark sewn with roots, even if awls of course may be used for many other purposes. Eighteen specimens are like Pl. 18.17-19, very slender and pointed in both ends. They correspond in shape and size with 39 specimens from the Ipiutak site classified as "Implements of Uncertain Use, Type 4" (Ipiutak: Pl. 28.15-16) and may belong in that category.

FLINT INDUSTRY

Taken as a whole, there are practically no inter-site differences between the material used for chipped stone implements, the types of implements, and the flaking tools from Deering and from Point

Hope. Hence for a detailed description, I refer to the text and illustrations in the Ipiutak Report.[144]

Flaking Tools

Only one hammer head was found at Deering. It is of antler, rounded-rectangular in cross section, and with a faint incision in each side for a lashing to the handle (Pl. 13.3).

There are two flaker handles of Ipiutak Type 1 in the collection, both of antler and both decorated with a pattern of incised lines. On the reverse side, there is a flat groove for a flaker point that had been held in place by a lashing supported by a flat knob on the lower side (Pl. 13.1-2). Regarding the decoration see figs. 33.a and b.

Pl. 13. 4-9 are six out of 13 flaker points found at Deering. They are made of walrus rib split length-wise with a smoothed upper side, while the lower side is unworked. They are more or less curved and range in length from 17.6 cm (Pl. 13.6) to 3.4 cm. The working end is in most cases rounded but three have a right slant, which is the most common on the Point Hope specimens. Four (e.g. Pl. 13.9) have a groove in the rear end while three are tapering (Pl. 13.5 and 8. Pl. 13.6). Another large piece has presumably been used without a handle.

Bifaced Blades

The flaking products fall naturally into two main categories, those chipped on two faces, here called blades, and these unifacially chipped. Of the first group, arrow points, inset blades, harpoon blades and the knife side blades inserted in their wooden handles have already been described.

In addition to the latter, there are eight more or less complete side blades and 31 blade fragments, a seemingly small number compared to the 361 complete side blades and 688 fragments found at Ipiutak. It should be kept in mind, however, that the large number is the result of the excavation of 72 houses and 138 burials; actually the number of knife blades found at Deering is more than the average for the Ipiutak houses at Point Hope.

Of the five blades illustrated in Plate 14, number 1 deviates from the majority of the Ipiutak side blades in having fine chipping along both edges instead of just one. According to the definition used in the Ipiutak report it should be classified as an end blade, but as mentioned there (p. 102) the classification of the end blades Type 1 and 2 is not too certain, and because one edge is thinner than the other, I am inclined to classify the Deering specimen as a side blade. Being slightly asymmetrical, it should be classified as Type 2. Pl. 14.2 is a typical side blade of brown flint with fine chipping along one edge and with large flakes taken off the other edge. This should also be classified as Type 2, while Pl. 14.3-5 being almost symmetrical, are closer to Type l. Pl. 14.3 of striated chalcedony is incomplete, but has fine chipping along what is left of one edge. Of the remaining three specimens, all of grey flint, one almost complete is of Type 2 and only 3.3 x 2.0 cm; the second though fragmentary, may be classified as Type 3, slender with a straight edge and a curved back, while the third is half of a long, slender blade unclassifiable as to type. Of the 31 fragments of side blades, 15 are of black flint, 14 of gray flint, 1 of brown flint, and one of chalcedony.

Plate 14.6 and 7 are the only two examples of bifacially chipped blades that in the Ipiutak report (page 101) are classified as semi lunar blades. Lacking secondary chipping along the edge they may be blanks. In the Ipiutak report, the semi lunar blades were interpreted as ulu blades assuming they had been hafted as the common Eskimo ulu or have had a wrapping around the back.[145] Now we can be fairly certain that the Ipiutak people did not use the ordinary ulu form but instead used knives with side blades for the same purpose. It is not unlikely that the semi lunar blades have been hafted as side blades and should be classified as such.

Discoidal Blades

Characteristic of the Deering flint industry is the relatively large number of discoidal blades. Except for Type 2, which is lacking, they may be classified as are those from Point Hope. Type 1, which is sub-quadrangular to oval in outline and with one convex, sharp edge, is represented by 11 spec-

---

[144] Ipiutak: 91-110 and Pl. 11.20.
[145] Ipiutak: 101.

imens (Pl. 14.13-16). They range in size from 5.1 x 4.2 cm to 3.4 x 2.7 cm and have an average thickness of 7.8 mm. They may have been hafted in a wooden handle like those found at Point Hope[146] and used as a blade inset in a two-handed scraper. The distinction between Type 1 and 3 is not always clear since both may be oval in outline. The criterion used is the extension of the secondary chipping of the edge. According to this, one specimen, Pl. 14.17, has been classified as Type 3, which is oval to elliptical in outline and with fine chipping along the entire margin or most of it. Type 4, circular in outline and with the same extension of the fine chipping along the edge as in Type 3, is represented by 9 specimens (Pl. 14.18-24). They range in size from 4 to 3 cm in diameter and average 7.2 cm in thickness. Type 3 and 4 were probably not hafted and I am inclined to believe that they were used for scraping rather than for cutting, some of them probably for scraping skin. Two unclassifiable fragments add to the number of discoidal blades in the collection.

Since the publication of the Ipiutak report, similar discoidal blades have found in Alaskan on other sites than Deering. They occur not only in other finds of Ipiutak culture but also in other assemblages. The most significant sites are the Norton layers at Cape Denbigh,[147] the Platinium Village Site,[148] Cape Krusenstern,[149] Onion Portage,[150] and the Hahanudan Lake Site in what is now Indian territory.[151] Their absence in finds from St. Lawrence Island and on the Asiatic side of the Bering Strait is worth noting.

Unifacially Chipped Flint Implements

Of the many thousand pieces of chert, jasper, silicified slate, and chalcedony, which I have chosen to call flint, and which numerically form by far the largest part of the collection brought back from Deering, only a small fraction (in all 484 pieces) show sign of having been used by man, the rest is undoubtedly waste from the production of imple-

ments. Of the 484 pieces 142 are complete or fragments of bifacially chipped implements. The remaining 342 constitute the group to be discussed under this heading. Of these the majority, namely 262 pieces, merely show sign of use in the form of retouch along one or more edges of the flake. The flakes are all different in shape and they vary in size from 9 x 11 cm to the size of a small fingernail.

They seem to fall into two groups. One consists of 139 specimens which have been retouched intentionally to be used for some purpose and then discarded. The retouch on the other 123 pieces is so faint that I do not think it was made on purpose, but that in these cases we are dealing with raw flakes that have been used as they were and have traces of use-wear as a result. The first of these groups have been designated retouched flakes; the second, used flakes. While there are not specimens alike in the two groups, the remaining 80 unifacially chipped implements lend themselves to classification into forms or types which admittedly are not well defined and probably of little significance regarding actual use. Nevertheless a classification is attempted here, in the first place for practical reasons and secondly because the same classification was used in the Ipiutak report.

Sidescrapers

With the exception of three, all 80 specimens fall within the category which in the Ipiutak report has been called sidescrapers.[152] The Deering specimens correspond in every respect to those from Point Hope. They consist of usually oblong flakes that along one or two margins are furnished with a more or less steep retouch made by pressure flaking. The retouch may be limited to the edges or it may cover most or all of the dorsal side of the flake, only in rare cases is the retouch found on the flat, ventral side.

The classification is based on whether the scraping edge is straight, concave or convex and whether there are one or two scraping edges. As at Point Hope, there is the difference between the single-edged and the double-edged scrapers. While there has been no attempt to give the former a definite shape, the double-edged are usu-

[146] Ipiutak: Pl. 22.16.
[147] Giddings 1964: 168.
[148] Larsen 1950: 184.
[149] Giddings and Anderson 1986.
[150] Giddings: pers. comm.
[151] Clark 1977: Pl. 9.
[152] Ipiutak: 105-108, fig. 24, and Pl. 16 and 17.

ally more carefully made with extended chipping of the dorsal side of the flake. In most cases, this gives them a shape characteristic of a number of specimens with the same kind of scraping edge.

In other words, they give the impression of being permanent tools in contrast to the single-edged, which like the retouched flakes were probably only used for a limited period of time. The only difference between the single-edged scrapers and the retouched flakes is that the scraping edge of the former is steeper and seems in general to have been more carefully made than that of the retouched flakes, but the distinction between the two is in many cases a matter of interpretive choice.

It is worth noting that Giddings, in his description of the Norton and Denbigh Flint Complex materials from Cape Denbigh, used the term sidescrapers only in connection with a number of "in nearly all cases crude flakes that have been treated along one edge – and sometimes more than one – from the Norton culture".[153] These "plano-convex scrapers" correspond largely to the Ipiutak single-edged sidescrapers and to some extent to retouched flakes. Other Ipiutak sidescrapers and gravers, primarily double-edged, which occur in almost identical forms in both the Norton and the Denbigh Flint culture, Giddings has designated as flakeknives.[154] Disregarding the difference in terminology because the specimens in question obviously were used for the same purpose, references will be made to the Cape Denbigh flakeknives as if they were sidescrapers.

With the reservation made above, the 77 sidescrapers may be classified as follows: 20 specimens, ranging in size from 6.9 x 1.8 cm (Pl. 15.5) to 3.9 x 1.8 cm have one concave scraping edge (Pl. 15.1-5). Five specimens have been chipped on the ventral side. Pl. 15.6-10 represent sidescrapers with one more or less straight scraping edge. The 21 specimens vary considerably in shape and they range in size from 6.1 x 4.1 cm to 3.1 x 1.5 cm. In addition to the scraping edge, some of the specimens have minor retouch along one or more mar-

gins. Only the four specimens illustrated in Pl. 15.11-14 constitute the group with a convex scraping edge, a group that at Point Hope exceeded the straight-edged in numbers.

As it appears from Pl. 15.15-19, the scrapers with chipping on two concave margins are very uniform in shape and size. Two additional pieces are fragmentary, one is thick like the specimens illustrated, the other is made of a thin flake. With the exception of the latter, they are all treated on the upper surface with the intention of giving them a definite form. One (Pl. 15.19) deviates from the rest by having a symmetrical "base" while the others have an asymmetrical "base" in relation to the long axis. This type, as we may rightly call it, does not occur in the finds from Cape Denbigh.

Nine specimens are like Pl. 16.1-6, chipped on a concave and a convex margin and with the exception of no. 1, 4, and 5, all have been treated on the upper surface as well. They range in length from 5.9 to 3.9 cm. On Pl. 16.2, 4, 5, and 6 the concave margin seems to have been chipped with greater care than the convex which raises the question of the function of these scrapers. In my opinion it is very likely that these specimens, and possibly all in this group, actually are concave sidescrapers and that the treatment of the convex edge only serves as trimming. One specimen in particular leads to this conclusion, namely Pl. 16.6. It is a typical example of the concave sidescraper with a tang or handle as found from Alaska to Greenland, but strangely enough it is the first example from the Ipiutak culture. In Alaska, the type occurs in the Denbigh Flint complex[155] and in the Old Bering Sea culture,[156] in Canada in Pre-Dorset as well as in Dorset sites[157], and in Greenland particularly in the Sarqaq culture, but also in Dorset assemblages.[158] There is no indication that the Deering specimen has been hafted like some of those from Greenland.

Nine specimens (e.g. Pl. 16.7-12) have a concave and a straight scraping edge. There is a considerable variation in shape and execution from slender and nicely chipped (7) to thin flakes without surface treatment (10). That the shape of the two edges is intentional is evident from Pl. 16.10-12,which shows three thin flakes with the concave edges chipped from the ventral side and the straight edge from the dorsal side. They vary in length from 7.4 to 4.8 cm.

[153] Giddings 1964: 167 and Pl. 55.
[154] Giddings 1964: Pl. 54 and 69.
[155] Giddings 1964: Pl. 69.15.
[156] Collins 1937: Pl. 41.22.
[157] Taylor 1968: figs. 18.a-b and 26.r and s.
[158] Larsen and Meldgaard 1958: 54, Pl. 2.10-12 and Pl. 3.18-22.

Only two short specimens, Pl. 16.13 and 14, have a straight and a convex scraping edge. No. 14 has the straight edge chipped from the ventral side, the convex from the dorsal.

Pl. 16.15-18 are four of the five sidescrapers with two straight edges. They are uniform in shape, size, and treatment of the upper surface, indicating that we are dealing with a definite type of artifact which is part of a permanent toolkit. Several of the so-called flakeknives from the Norton layer of Cape Denbigh are very similar to these scrapers.[159]

Other Unifacially Chipped Flint Implements

Two specimens, Pl. 16.19 and 20, chipped on three margins and forming one or two points may be classified as pointed scrapers, a term used for two specimens from Point Hope[160] although it is questionable whether they should be grouped together. Pl. 16.19 has three concave, retouched margins meeting in two sharp points, which might have been used for drilling. Retouch covers most of the upper surface. Pl. 16.20 has two concave, chipped margins meeting in a point; the third margin is straight and chipped from the reverse side. It is uncertain whether these two specimens were used as scrapers or borers or both.

Pl. 16.21 corresponds in shape and size to the endscrapers of type 2 from Point Hope.[161] It is a thin flake with a steep scraping edge in one end and faint retouch on part of the long margins. Pl. 16.22 may be classified as an endscraper with a right slanting scraping edge in front and retouch on one side (compare with Ipiutak Pl. 18.11-15).

Pl. 16.23 is very similar to gravers of type 2 from Point Hope.[162] It is a thin, curved flake with faint retouch on both margins and a sharp point.

In addition to the specimens mentioned above, the collection contains 16 fragments of unclassifiable, unifacially chipped flint tools, most of them sidescrapers. There also are a number of blanks and cores; none of the latter may be identified as

prepared cores. In connection with cores, it should be mentioned that in the collections there is a small, oval and rather flat core of obsidian and 11 small, irregular chips of the same material.

HOUSEHOLD UTENSILS

As one could expect, the find contains no lamps or cooking pots of stone or clay which means that the fireplace was the only source of heat and light and that cooking must have taken place by the use of hot stones in containers of wood, bark, or skin. The only indication of the use of wooden containers is the tiny fragment of a rim illustrated in Pl. 19.3, which may be part of a bowl. Pl. 19.1 and 2 are two more or less complete, oblong wooden trays, which may have been used for serving food. The larger, which has a thin, black crust on the inside, is 1.7 cm thick, the smaller is 0.9 cm. Both are made of spruce, as are 21 fragments probably of similar trays ranging in size from 27 x 13.8 cm to 4.7 x 1.8 cm and all about the same thickness. The largest piece has many marks of cutting on the inside; another large piece has a black crust.

The finding of pieces of birch bark with rows of small holes in two of the Point Hope houses made us believe that the Ipiutak people had used "containers with a round or oval wooden bottom and with vertical sides made of a rectangular piece of birch bark bent around the bottom, similar to those used by most Eskimo but made with thin wooden or baleen walls."[163] Of the numerous pieces of worked birch bark that we found in and particularly just outside the Deering house, a considerable number had rows of small holes near the edges like the pieces from Point Hope, hence it seemed as we had here ample support of our assumption regarding bark containers. Of the samples of worked pieces of birch bark illustrated in Pl. 20, nos. 3 and 4 are of the kind just discussed. Of these Pl. 20.3, one of the largest pieces of bark in the collection, is cut on all four sides and has about 20 small holes along each of the long edges. In some of the holes are pieces of the willow root lines with which it has been sewn. The inside of the bark, which is shown in the illustration, is partly covered by a thin, black crust. This piece as well as Pl. 20.4 and several others, some with remains of a black crust on the inner

[159] Giddings 1964: Pl. 54.
[160] Ipiutak: Pl. 20.7.
[161] Ipiutak: Pl. 18.6-10.
[162] Ipiutak: Pl. 19.7-12.
[163] Ipiutak: 111.

side of the bark, may have been parts of containers for cooking, but as we shall see shortly, this is not the only possibility. One reason for questioning the interpretation of them as parts of containers with vertical walls and round or oval wooden bottoms is the fact that despite the perfect state of preservation, we did not find a single complete bottom nor any fragments that could be interpreted as such. In other words there is little left in support of our original assumption of the kind of bark containers used by the Ipiutak people.

There is, however, another possibility, namely that they have used bark containers of the "folded" type as those used by the Athapaskans, and though a definite proof is lacking there is in my opinion good reason to believe that this is the case. This statement is based on the specimen illustrated in Pl. 20.1. It consists of three pieces of bark stitched together with willow root lines. The wide piece at the bottom is actually 30 cm long but it is folded three times so only less than half its length is shown in the illustration. At the top it is sewn onto a 4-4.4 cm wide piece of thicker bark the direction of which is at right angle to the former. This second, horizontal, piece is reinforced on the back with a third strip of rather thick bark sewn on with stitches in two rows. The bark of this third strip, which is actually made of two pieces, is in the same direction as the wide piece at the bottom and its upper end is tightly rolled around the top forming the bead visible along the upper edge.

The specimen described above is reminiscent of the birch bark baskets from the Ingalik as described and illustrated by Cornelius Osgood.[164] Although our specimen is much coarser than any of the baskets illustrated by Osgood, it seems reasonable to assume that it is a rim section of a similar basket. My interpretation is mainly based on the presence of the horizontal strip of thick bark and the bead along the upper edge. In comparison, the berry basket of the Ingalik has "a reinforcing strip of birch bark all the away around the top edge", and in the detailed description of the making of the water baskets it is mentioned that the edges of the birch bark baskets are made of two

thicknesses of birch bark. The bead along the edge of our specimen probably corresponds to the wrapping of the edge of most of these types of baskets and which in some cases is connected with a beading of the edge. The Deering specimen has the following significant traits in common with the Ingalik "birch bark boiling basket": in the first place "the workmanship is extremely rough" and, secondly, "the most distinctive feature of all is the fact that the outside of the birch bark forms the inner side of the basket – the only case when it occurs", and finally, it lacks the reinforcement with a stick of cranberry wood with which the other forms of baskets are provided. The Ingalik basket has no edging and is made of very thick bark, while the lower part of our specimen is made of thin, relatively pliable bark. The latter difference makes it questionable whether the two were used for the same purpose. The Ingalik basket was usually made by men when they wanted to boil something and no women were around,[165] in other words a sort of an emergency basket. It was hung over a low burning fire and by being careful they could bring the liquid in the basket "approximately to a boiling point without setting fire to the birch bark". Whether or not our specimen has been used as a boiling basket is questionable. On one hand the bark is blackened on the outside, which speaks in favor, on the other hand it seems to me that the bark is too thin to stand such treatment. Unfortunately, it is the only specimen of its kind in the collection, which means that the interpretation is not absolutely certain. Consequently, I prefer to leave the question open. Pl. 20.2, which might be another rim section of a container, consists of one piece of bark folded at the top to form a 5.3-6.3 cm wide double layer along the upper edge. The two layers have been sewn together as indicated by a horizontal row of small holes 2 cm below the edge. Similar holes also occur at each end, some of them with remains of willow root lines. It is the inside of the bark that has formed the outside of the supposed container.

Assuming that bark containers of the folded type were the only kind used, we must look for another explanation for the bark pieces with rows of holes like those mentioned above and illustrated in Pl. 20.3 and 4. A large piece like that in Pl. 20.3 could have been used as the rectangular pieces inserted in an Ingalik berry basket as illus-

[164] Osgood 1940: 133-142.
[165] Osgood 1940: 142.

trated by Osgood.[166] The smaller piece, Pl. 20.4, may, if it is not part of a container, belong to an entirely different category to be described below. But first Pl. 20.5 deserves mentioning. It consists of very thick birch bark the outside of which is shown in the illustration. The close-set, rounded holes near the left edge are quite different in shape and arrangement from the sewing holes in other pieces of birch bark in the collection. I have no suggestion to offer regarding its use.

In Pl. 20.6 two oblong pieces of thin birch bark are sewn together with a double, thin root line. The stitches are similar to those used on the Ingalik berry basket mentioned above. On the reverse side is a black crust, which could be remains of food.

The majority of the cut and sewn pieces of birch bark in the collection are, however, not part of containers but have served an entirely different purpose. Pl. 20.7 is the largest of a number of similar pieces. It consists of five pieces of bark sewn together with rather thick willow root lines. In the middle are two large pieces, 34 cm long and 22-17 cm wide, one on top of the other and both with the inner side of the bark turned out. Sewn to either end are smaller pieces, undoubtedly fragments of pieces like those in the middle; in other words the illustrated specimen is apparently a fragment of a strip of birch bark consisting of two layers of bark with the inside out and made up of at least three sections probably of the size of the middle one. Other pieces of bark in the collection have approximately the same dimensions as the middle pieces of the illustration, namely about 30 x 20 cm, indicating that it is the standard size of the sections. We cannot be sure, but it is possible that the length of the sections also gives us an idea of the size of the trees from which the bark was taken. According to this the trunk of the trees should not have been much more than 10 cm thick.

Before we try to figure out what these strips of bark have been used for, it should be made clear that of the 260 pieces of worked birch bark that were registered, not less than 206 were found outside the house, and in section B east of the house,

while only 32 pieces were found inside the house. It is also worth noting that by making the sheets double and placing the two pieces with the inside out, they prevented them from curling as well as made them stronger. The fact that they were intended to be flat and that they were found outside the house seems to me to indicate that they may have been used on the roof and that the roof had been removed, possibly temporarily in connection with an airing of the house.

The use of birch bark as roofing material in Alaska is to my knowledge only mentioned a couple of times and the method of making strips of two layers of bark not at all. From the Bering Sea area Nelson mentions that the roof is "covered with slabs or planks over which pieces of bark are laid",[167] and from the Tanaina we have greater detail. According to Osgood, the use of birch bark as roof covering is a point of difference between the area of upper Cook Inlet and the Kenai and Kachemak Bay areas, as it is used in the former area but not in the latter. From Tyonek he has the interesting information, "that the native term for winter house (nícil) ancient referred to strips of birch bark strengthened by having other strips sewn on the edges, and that these were used in as coverings in constructing a shelter".[168] Also the Iliamna people sew strips of birch bark together (with spruce roots) for a special cover for a semi-spherical lodge. Finally, about the Upper Inlet summer house or smoke house in general: "Sides and roof the Indians construct by placing strips of birch bark over a framework of poles. They lay the bark on horizontally, alternating the side of the bark up so that the edges curl over and lock. Willow poles laid on top provide additional support".[169]

Though I believe that the Deering bark sheets have been used as roofing material, I do not think it was the only material used to cover the roof. In the first place, a roof of that size would require an enormous amount of birch bark which had to be transported a long distance and which apparently only was available in relatively small pieces; secondly, as roofing material it was probably not warm enough in the winter. Hence, I am inclined to believe that it has been used in connection with moss turf or sod, which in that case would constitute the main roofing material, while the bark probably was used for closing holes or leaks.

---

[166] Osgood 1940: 136.
[167] Nelson 1899: 248.
[168] Osgood 1937: 61.
[169] Osgood 1937: 62-63.

whipping consists of grass. As the top of most of the stitches is bifurcated, it is the kind of work which Otis T. Mason calls furcate coil.[170] It also occurs on the pieces of coiled basketry from the Platinum Village Site.[171] Coiled basketry is still being made by the Alaskan Eskimos from the Bering Sea coast and at least as far north as Point Hope. Coiled baskets similar to some made in Alaska are also known from the Koryak and other people in Siberia, and de Laguna has expressed the opinion that "whatever the history of coiled baskets, there is no doubt that those of the Eskimo, Tena, Koryak, Kamchadal and Ainu are closely related.[172]

Grass Matting

Figure 31 is part of a grass mat that was lying on the platform in the southwest corner of the third layer of the main room. It consisted of 3-4 cm thick bundles of grass connected by twining with thinner bundles of the same kind of grass. Grass matting, though thinner, has been illustrated by de Laguna from the Tena,[173] by Oswalt from Hooper Bay[174] and by Giddings from Nukleet in Norton Sound.[175] In all those cases however, the mats are of a much finer texture than the Deering specimen, which was so loose that it is not meant to be taken up and moved around.

Spoons and ladles

Four specimens, Pl. 21.1-4, have been classified as spoons although their bowl is so flat that they cannot hold much, at least little that is liquid. Pl. 21.1-2 is rather crudely made of antler and has an indication of a pierced handle. Pl. 21.3 is made of ivory and has an interesting characteristic ornament on the back of the bowl which will be discussed later. Pl. 21.4 is of antler and is flat on both sides. The classification of it as a spoon is a tentative suggestion. Only two small antler spoons were found at Point Hope. It is also questionable whether the four specimens illustrated in Pl.

Pl. 20.8 is a roll of rather thick birch bark wrapped around a wooden stick, undoubtedly for transportation. The width of the bark is 35 cm, the same as the rectangular piece illustrated in Pl. 20.3. In the collection there are three other sticks wrapped with birch bark but they are much shorter and have probably nothing to do with transportation of the bark.

Basketry

Two small pieces of coiled basketry were found (Pl. 21.17 and 18). The foundation as well as the

---

[170] Mason 1904: 244.
[171] Larsen 1950: fig. 57.
[172] de Laguna 1947: 219.
[173] de Laguna 1947: Pl. XIX.
[174] Oswalt 1952: Pl. 8.
[175] Giddings 1964: fig. 18.

Fig. 32: Fire-drill and hearth from SW corner of Qalegi *(photo L. Larsen).*

21. 7-10 should be placed in this category, but like the spoons mentioned above, they have a handle and a flat "bowl". Pl. 21.8 is of antler, the rest of wood.

Fire Drills

The Deering find contains a culture element which strangely enough is absent in the Ipiutak find from Point Hope. Although the preservation of wood was poor, one could expect to find charred wood which is always better preserved than fresh wood. Despite the absence of fire drills at Point Hope we must assume that fire drilling was used there too. No less than 13 fire drills and 13 hearths were found at Deering. The drills, all made of spruce, vary considerably in execution and length. Plate 19.8 is distinguished by its unusual length, 64.5 cm, and a rather coarse surface treatment. The diameter just above the rounded, charred butt is 2.5 cm. The upper, pointed end shows no sign of wear. One other

---

[176] Hough 1892: 395 and fig. 51.

specimen, 42 cm long and 2.2 cm in diameter near the conical, charred butt, has the same rough surface; the remainder have a more or less smooth surface. They vary in length from 17 to 34.5 cm and from 1.8 to 2.3 cm in diameter (Pl. 19.4-7). They are all charred on the conical or rounded butt and most of them are also charred at the top, which brings us to the question of how they were used.

From the material at hand, it seems that more than one method has been used. The longest drill, Pl. 19.8, and the few others that are not charred at the top must have been twirled with the hands alone, in other words the simplest method of fire drilling, the two-part hand drill.[176] The majority of the drills are charred at the top, and five of them are conical as a result of rotation, as they must have been used with a mouthpiece or a handrest, as we know it from the Eskimos. No mouthpieces were found at Deering, but the willow stick in fig. 32 could have served as a handrest. It has two circular holes, one in each end, similar to those in the hearths to be described below but only 1.3 cm in diameter in contrast to those in the hearths, which average 2.5 cm. This, however, is the only piece in the collection that could have served as a handrest. The Eskimos also use a cord with their fire drill, either attached to a bow or with a handle in each end, but there is nothing in the find to indicate the use of a cord in connection with fire making. There are no drill bows, nothing that could be interpreted as handles for a cord, and no sign of wear by a cord on any of the well-preserved drills. From this we must conclude that the drill was rotated with the palms of the hands with or without the use of a handrest, which is more like Indian than Eskimo practice.

The collection contains 12 hearths of spruce with one or more circular depressions produced as a result of fire making. There are depressions as wide as 3 cm in diameter, but most of them are about 2.5 cm. Pl. 19.11 is an unusually solid piece of wood for this purpose. It is 6.3 cm wide and 6.8 cm thick and worked on four sides. A V-shaped groove runs through the entire length of the piece connecting the holes, a feature which occurs on some of the other specimens (e.g. Pl. 19.10), and which is essential for the collection of the wood dust produced by the rotation of the drill. Actually the groove is probably made first and the holes then made in the groove. Pl. 19.9 shows a fragment of a hearth with a V-shaped groove roughened in two places where the holes are going to be bored.

Pl.19.11 is a lump of pyrites probably used for making fire, indicating that both methods were known and used at Deering.

CLOTHING AND PERSONAL ADORNMENT

The number of specimens that may be classified as parts of costumes or personal adornment is extremely small. Pl. 22.6 is one of three fragments of wooden snow goggles, which apparently had oblong holes for the eyes. Five specimens, Pl. 22.1-5, have been identified as fragments of thin bands of antler and ivory that may have been used for personal adornment. Nos. 1-4 may be brow bands like those from Point Hope[177] and no. 5 (of ivory) is reminiscent of the decorated bands illustrated

[177] Ipiutak: Pl. 24. 15-21.
[178] VanStone and Lucier 1974.
[179] Ipiutak: fig. 29.

in Ipiutak, fig. 38. Of other ornamental objects from Deering, Pl. 22.7 seems to be a bead of ivory with a wide perforation, Pl. 22.8 a large pendant of ivory, and Pl. 22.17 a small button of ivory. On the reverse side, which is flat, a bar divides the eyehole in two.

A pendant of antler carved in the shape of a human face was found by a resident of Deering some time after our excavation and "in the immediate vicinity of the *qalgei*" so "It is presumed, on stylistic grounds and proximity of location, to have come from this structure". The quotations are from a publication by James W. VanStone and Charles V. Lucier, the latter of which obtained the specimen in 1951.[178] The main reason for mentioning it here is that the face besides showing tattooing had a round hole at the corner of the mouth probably for an inset, indicating the use of labrets. This is significant because no labrets were found at Deering.

Another example of tattooing is the flat wooden stick illustrated by Pl. 23.7, which shows a schematic face very much like one on an antler tube from Burial 21 at Point Hope.[179] Both have a Y-shaped nose line, two eyes, and four horizontal cheek lines on each side of the nose. Instead of indications of labrets, the Deering specimen has five lines on the chin.

ART

Though relatively few in number, the examples of art in the find from Deering conform by and large to the art of the Ipiutak culture, as we know it from Point Hope. It is particularly true of the decorative art in the form of incised lines on artifacts of antler and ivory. These range from the simple line decoration on arrowheads, barbed prongs, harpoon heads, and foreshafts to more intricate patterns. The most elaborately decorated harpoon head, fig. 19a and Pl. 2.6, is reminiscent of the harpoon heads of Type 2 from Point Hope as illustrated in Ipiutak, fig. 13, and in particular fig. 13g. A difference worthy of note is the presence on the Deering specimen of five tiny round insets, probably of ivory, two placed symmetrically on the "back" and two "in front" and one in the wide belt, a unique feature on the "back". The pattern on the harpoon head type 3, fig. 19b and Pl. 2.9,

Fig. 33: Ornamented flaker handles, (a) is 16.4 cm long (drawings J. Rosing).

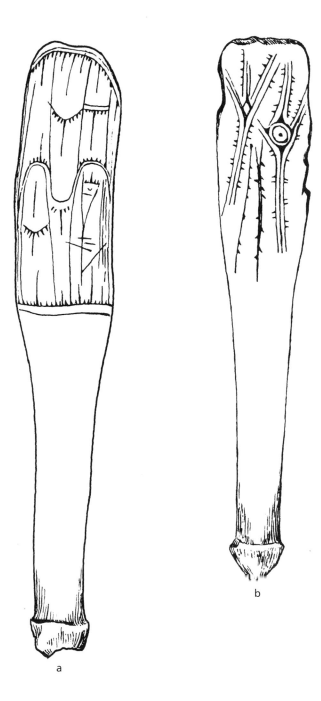

a

b

may not be duplicated but the Point Hope specimens of the same type (Ipiutak: fig. 42) show corresponding elements like the broken lines and the nucleated circle. The decoration of the harpoon socket piece fig. 20 has already been described. Both flaker handles found at Deering are decorated (figs. 33.a and b). Though different in style, both decorations may be attributed to the art of the Ipiutak culture, thus the decoration on fig. 33.a is reminiscent of that on a flaker handle from House 32 at Point Hope (Ipiutak: fig. 19 c.d.), and there is a close resemblance between the pattern on fig. 33.b and that of the decorated band from Burial 61 (Ipiutak: fig. 38a). A pattern similar to that on the flaker handle from House 32 (although more refined and elaborate) occurs, on the back of the spoon Pl. 21.2. Noteworthy are the extremely fine lines that interspace the heavy lines of the main motif.

Not conforming to any known form of Ipiutak decoration is the coarse straight-line decoration on the obverse side of the flat piece of antler illustrated in Pl. 23.8 and the decoration on birch bark, Pl. 23.11. Plate 23.10 is a fragment of a wooden board, 1.1 cm thick and painted black on both sides and with three red lines on the obverse side. The find contains other pieces of wood painted black, and traces of red paint may be seen on the schematic face, Pl. 23.7 and on the decorative band, Pl. 22.5.

There are not many examples of sculptural art in the find, but most of them are reminiscent of similar pieces from Point Hope. A good example is the harpoon socket piece fig. 20 and Pl. 2.14. Most socket pieces from Point Hope Ipiutak are carved in the shape of animal heads, but one specimen (Ipiutak: Pl. 25.1) is anthropomorphic. Like the Deering specimen it is of antler, it has the same round eye sockets, the same wide nose, and a large mouth, which is turned down and not slanting. The Deering specimen, which is described in detail previously, also shows points

of similarity with another socket piece from Point Hope (Ipiutak: Pl. 6.1).

The two ends of throwing sticks, figs. 21 and 22 and Pl. 4.15 and 18, are examples of one of the characteristics of Ipiutak art, namely "the frequent use of realistic and fantastic animal heads as terminal decoration on many kinds of artifacts".[180] As already mentioned the head on fig. 21 probably represents that of a seal while the other head must refer to the realm of fantasy. To the same category belong the primitive, similar indications of animal heads on two of the wooden handles Pl. 25

---

[180] Ipiutak: 145.

and the wooden head Pl. 23.4, which seems to have been part of a larger object.

Plate 23.5 is the only carving representing a whole animal, a seal carved in ivory with two round eye sockets for insets and a slot at the throat very much like seal figures found at Point Hope (Ipiutak: Pl. 25.6-10 and Pl. 52.6-8). In the find there is also an example, though quite primitive, of a part of an animal, in this case representing a caribou leg (Pl. 23. 6), a motive also known from Point Hope (Ipiutak: Pl. 51.7 and Pl. 52.12). Pl. 22.13 is a small carving of an unidentifiable animal head. It is of antler and apparently unfinished. Another antler carving representing part of an animal head is shown in Pl. 22.15. It probably represents the upper part of a seal or walrus head; the reverse side is concave and the carving is in this respect reminiscent of the carvings of small human heads from Point Hope Ipiutak (Pl. 25.2-11). Of the decoration on the obverse side the hachure at the top is noticeable because hachure is rarely used in Ipiutak art. The unusual carving in ivory, Pl. 22.14, seems to be complete but the meaning of it is obscure. The backside is flat and undecorated and it can stand on the two wide knobs at the bottom. On the other hand, if it is turned upside-down it might show a wide mouth and four cheek lines of a schematic face, but in that case we lack an explanation for the two knobs.

The three pieces of wood with the roughly marked human features (P1. 23.1-3) may not come under the category of art and may be the work of children, but they are interesting because they show something universal. From Point Hope we have the same crude human features on a wedge-shaped piece of antler (Ipiutak: Pl. 25.5). Finally, the meaning of the wooden carving with the eight encircling lines (Pl. 23.9) is obscure.

MISCELLANEOUS OBJECTS

In addition to the categories of artifacts described in the foregoing the Deering find contains a considerable number of objects which do not naturally fall within these categories. Some of these objects are represented by two or more specimens that are so much alike that it is reasonable to assume that they were used for the same purpose

and may be considered as a type, others occur as only one specimen. Some of the objects are identifiable as to their former use, but the great majority must be classified as implements of uncertain use. The number of unidentifiable objects is particularly large due to the unusually good preservation of wood and other perishable materials which has resulted in a great many objects that occur here for the first time. References will be made to the miscellaneous objects in the Ipiutak find from Point Hope which in the Ipiutak Report are briefly described in the text accompanying Plates 26-31 and 75-76.

One half of an *antler tube* (Pl. 21.5) was found in two pieces, one east and one west of the house. It is 9.9 cm long and has a lashing groove at each end. Eleven antler tubes were found at Point Hope, five in houses and six in burials, most of them long and curved and decorated with incised lines. One specimen, Ipiutak Pl. 26.18, is of about the same shape and size as the Deering specimen. The Ipiutak antler tubes have tentatively been interpreted as trinket boxes.

Three lumps of ferruginous minerals, each of them with a rubbed surface (Pl. 21.12-14) have probably been used for *paint*. Traces of red paint are found on one of the rubbed surfaces of Pl. 21.6, a piece of graywacke, which has been used for sharpening needles. The pumice (Pl. 21.11) has been used for the same purpose and possibly also for polishing other objects and perhaps in skin-dressing.

Plate 24.18 is a *hook* rather coarsely made from antler and with the lower end broken off. The 17 hooks found in the Ipiutak houses at Point Hope (Pl. 27.1-5) were all different in size and shape. *Swivels* and swivel-like objects, one of the characteristic elements in the Ipiutak find from Point Hope, are only represented by one, fragmentary specimen of antler (Pl. 24.19). Because the bearing for the rotating shaft is broken it is impossible to identify it as to type. The small perforation and the narrow groove for a thin line on both sides at the top distinguish it from most of the swivels from Point Hope.

The *stone sinker* illustrated in Pl. 24.21 is the only one of its kind known from Ipiutak finds and may be intrusive. It has a single, rather narrow line-groove all around the long axis.

Plate 21.15 is an object consisting of a *four-strand*

plait of willow root which when found was connected to the wooden stick wrapped with willow root below. Similar objects but made of baleen instead of willow root are known from Old Bering Sea culture on St. Lawrence Island,[181] from Birnirk as well as later cultures of the Barrow region[182] and from the Thule culture in Greenland 3.[183] In the National Museum there are three examples of four-strand plaits of willow root from the Copper Eskimos at Coronation Gulf collected by the Canadian Arctic Expedition 1913-18. One is of the same dimension as the Deering specimen, the other two are of different length and thickness. They are labeled as "Children's toys of plaited willow" by Diamond Jenness. The ring shown in Pl. 21.16 is made up of several strands of willow root wrapped with the same material.

In the Ipiutak report the *implements of uncertain use* are classified into 15 types plus the specimens of which only one example was found. Of the 8 types that also occur in this find, Type 1 has already been described as "Blunt Arrowheads". It is noticeable that Type 2 (with 32 specimens) is not represented in the Deering find. Type 3, however, is even more numerous than at Point Hope. They are thin, hollow bird bones cut straight at one or both ends and with notches or a transverse groove near one end (Pl. 24.1-5). The 42 specimens vary in length from 12.1 cm (Pl. 24.1) to 3.7 cm (Pl. 24.3). The majority is made of goose radii, two of goose ulna, one of auk ulna (Pl. 24.4), and one of auk humerus (Pl. 24.5). Six specimens have from one to five short, transverse lines on the shaft, possibly the owner's marks. In the Ipiutak report, these bird bones have been interpreted as "possibly parts of squirrel snare" (Pl. 28.12-14). That they were part of a snare is undoubtedly correct because we know from Nelson that "cylinders made from the hollow wing-bones of birds" were used for snares at the head of Kotzebue Sound.[184] The snares could very well have been used for ground squirrels which are common in that region. Considering the large number of these bird bones found, snaring of ground squirrels

must have played an important role. The extensive use of goose bones also as material for needles is noteworthy.

Implements of uncertain use, *type 4* are illustrated in Pl. 18.17-19. Eighteen specimens, 15 made from antler and, three from ivory, are slender shafts pointed at both ends and ranging in size from 14.5 cm to 6.5 cm (Pl. 18.18). Probably some and maybe all of them have been used as awls, but they may have served other purposes as well. Thirty-nine specimens of this type were found at Point Hope.[185]

The implements of uncertain use, *type 5* are puzzling. They are described in the Ipiutak report (Pl. 28.17-23) as "wedge-shaped to conical ivory or antler objects with flat top and curved or straight transverse edge". They are puzzling because they look like small wedges but have probably not been used as such. The majority are of walrus ivory (at Point Hope 23 ivory and 2 antler, at Deering 6 ivory and 5 antler), and most are carefully made with smooth, polished surfaces that in many cases are decorated. Four of the Point Hope specimens are decorated with two to four incised, equally spaced, longitudinal lines or grooves, and two of the Deering specimens has the same decoration. The Deering specimens (Pl. 24.10-13) range in length from 9.4 cm (Pl. 24.10) to 2.3 cm (Pl. 24.13). They seem to be a tool that was held in the hand with the edge in the lower end as the working part. This at least seems to be the function of Pl. 24.10 the lower end of which is much worn. The oblique edge is suggestive of another type of implement of uncertain use, namely *Type 15*, which in the Ipiutak report is described as: "ivory objects, with rounded or oblique sharp edge in one end" (Pl. 29.8,9). In the present material, 12 specimens have been classified as belonging to this type. Of these six are of ivory, five of antler, and one of wood; they range in length from 13.2 cm to 7.1 cm (Pl. 24. 14-17). Except for the working edge, which may be rounded, oblique or straight, the specimens do not have much in common. Three are made from barbed prongs and two apparently from arrowhead blanks. Two specimens of ivory have (like Pl. 24.17) notches or grooves in the proximal end as if they have been hafted, perhaps like a mattock. If so they belong in another category.

Implements of uncertain use, *Type 6* are reminis-

[181] Collins 1937: Pl. 56.8-9.
[182] Ford 1959: 230 and fig. 11.
[183] Holtved 1944: 288 and Pl. 49.20.
[184] Nelson 1899: 124 and Pl. LI.4.
[185] Ipiutak: Pl. 28.15-16.

cent of Type 15 and yet they form a distinct group. In the Ipiutak report they are described as: "Bones with flat, worked point", but in addition to five specimens made of various bones, one made of ivory is included (Pl. 29.1). The collection from Deering contains five specimens that have been classified as Type 6 (Pl. 18.20-24). Only two are made of bone, Pl. 18.20 of a caribou ulna and Pl. 18.21 of a dog tibia, of the others two are of antler and, one of ivory. The reason for classifying them as one type is the shape of the point, which is flat, pointed, and with sharp edges. Pl. 18.23 is a reworked harpoon foreshaft. The points are very smooth as a result of wear. I am inclined to interpret this type as well as Type 15 as women's tools used in connection with dressing skins for clothing. The bone specimens of Type 6 are reminiscent of a "bone boot crimper" of lynx ulna from the Ingalik,[186] and some of the Type 15 specimens could have been used for a similar purpose.

The flat, ring-shaped objects with a projection illustrated in Pl. 24.6-8 are exactly like five specimens from Point Hope (Pl. 28.24-25) which are classified as implements of uncertain use, *Type 7*. Of the three specimens from Deering, two are of antler, one of ivory. A somewhat similar ivory object, though coarser and with an oblong perforation (Pl. 24.9), may belong in the same category, as does a blank. Regarding their use, we suggested in the Ipiutak report that they may be rings for belts or other parts of the costume.

Type 8, Implements of uncertain use, has already been described as hand protectors for bows because there can hardly be any doubt about that the first interpretation was correct (Ipiutak, Pl. 28.26-27 and p.68).

Plate 22.16 is an example of Implements of uncertain use, *Type 9* which in the Ipiutak report are described as flat, ivory objects with a deep notch near each end (Pl. 28.28 and 29). The specimen illustrated here is the only one found.

Plate 24.20 is reminiscent of Ipiutak Pl. 29.2, which is classified as Implements of uncertain use, *type 10*, "long, slender ivory or antler shafts, with an eyehole in one end". The present specimen is of antler, almost square at the eyehole and pointed at the other end. It could have been used as a trout

needle as suggested in the Ipiutak report, if such were used.

Plate 24.22 is undoubtedly another example of what in the Ipiutak report is described as Implements of uncertain use, *Type 12* (Pl. 29.5), though the "type" consisted of only one specimen. The fact that another specimen has turned up shows that we are dealing with a distinct type. Like the Point Hope specimen it is made from ivory and has a distinct handle separated from the working end of the tool by a projection. Instead of a suspension hole, the handle terminates in a knob. The lower end, part of which is chopped off, is semi lunar in cross section and was probably tapered towards the point like the Point Hope specimen. The entire surface is covered by marks probably made with an adze, but they are much worn indicating that the tool has been used despite the unfinished appearance. It has been a tool that could withstand much strain but I am unable to make any suggestion regarding its use.

Of the four *ivory pegs* illustrated in Pl. 22.9-12, two with disc-shaped heads have counterparts at Point Hope (Pl. 27.13) except for the shape of the stems, which on the Point Hope specimens is pointed, on the present ones rounded or flat. Pl. 22.11 and 12 constitute a new type characterized by a round head with three indentations, two large, round ones representing eyes and possibly meant for inlays, and one representing a mouth. The stem of the larger specimen is pierced at the end. The use of the four pegs is unknown.

Hollow bones, primarily bird bones but also bones of small mammals, in which are inserted another, thinner bone, a thin, wooden shaft, or the shaft of a feather are known from various forms of Eskimo culture from Alaska to Greenland. *Inset bird* bones were also found in Ipiutak houses at Point Hope (Ipiutak Pl. 27.21), one of them with a pointed wooden shaft. In the Deering find are three short, broken bones, each of them with a wooden shaft inserted (Pl. 24.23). A Greenlander told Therkel Mathiassen that these inset bird bones in Greenland were used as toy weapons, possibly representing a harpoon socket piece and foreshaft.[187]

Miscellaneous wooden objects. As mentioned above, the Deering find contains an unusually large number of unidentified objects, which is due to the fact that so many objects, particularly of

[186] Osgood 1940: 88.
[187] Mathiassen 1931: 105.

wood, occur here for the first time. Before turning to the unidentified objects it should be mentioned that the two wooden pieces illustrated in Pl. 26.14-15 are most likely *amulet boxes*. No. 14 is a piece of an alder branch, one side of which is hollowed out; on the other, rounded, side is a faint impression probably of a binding for a lid. The hollow has a black coating of unknown origin. In shape and size it looks very much like amulet boxes found in various places between Alaska and East Greenland. Remains of bees in such boxes are reported from both areas.[188] The other specimen (Pl. 26.15) is cut out of a 2 cm thick piece of bark, probably of poplar like that used for the boat model.

Four wooden objects, each consisting of a short, perforated handle and a long, slender shaft (Pl. 25.1-4) constitute a definite type of artifact which also occur in the Ipiutak find from Point Hope (Ipiutak: Pl. 31.8). They are very carefully made, with a smooth surface which shows sign of wear, and the uniformity in shape and size is noticeable. It is an interesting fact that Pl. 25.1 and 2 are almost identical in handle shape and in total length, 41 cm. The shafts are elliptic in cross section and slightly curved and the handles concave with two transverse grooves on one side, convex and plain on the other. The other two, Pl. 25.3 and 4, are not complete but were probably also at one time almost identical. Although no.3 is split lengthwise we must assume that the handle like that of no.4 had two identical sides; at least both handles terminate with engraved eyes and a mouth, representing an animal head. No. 4 is made shorter with four cuts. It should be mentioned that a similar type of handle, though wider, occurs on two wooden knife handles (Pl. 10.2).

As mentioned above, the type also occurs in the Ipiutak collection from Point Hope. Four specimens are described as: "Curved wooden objects with a knob in one end", but the collection actually contains two additional specimens, namely an almost complete specimen, 35.5 cm long and 1.7 cm thick, with a slightly curved shaft and a perforated handle from House 4, and a handle reminiscent of the illustrated specimen from Ipiutak from

House 5. We thus have a total of 10 specimens that we must assume have been used for the same purpose, but what purpose? They are so carefully made and so uniform that one's first thoughts go in direction of a ceremonial object and if there were indications of the presence of drums in the Ipiutak culture a drum stick would be the obvious answer, but not the slightest evidence has been found so far. Unable to find another possible ceremonial use, I wonder if they are of a more practical nature, and suggest that they are *snow beaters*, used for beating snow off clothing and other things made from fur. Snow beaters of wood of approximately the same length as ours and with rounded edges and a handle with a knob in the end are, according to Therkel Mathiassen with reference to the Igulik Eskimos, "indispensable household utensils – with which clothing must be beaten as soon as one comes inside the house, as otherwise the snow will soon melt".[189] Curved and straight examples of snow beaters of bone, ivory, and antler were in use in Alaska in historical times.[190]

Plate 25.5-9 are five *wooden handles* for unidentified implements of which at least nos. 5 and 6 are part of the same implement and nos. 8 and 9 may be part of the same. Nos. 5 and 6 have three traits in common, a distinct flatter and wider proximal end, an oblong perforation through the widest part, and a longitudinal groove (clearly visible on Pl. 25.6) along what seems to be the back of the handle. Nos. 8 and 9 share two features, an elliptical cross section and an oblong perforation through the thin part. Pl. 25.7 is somewhat of a reminiscent of the latter two.

Plate 25.10 and 11 are apparently fragments of *splice- pieces* though not necessarily used for the same purpose. Both have one flat surface, which has been spliced to some unknown object and held in place by one or more lashings. In Pl. 25.10 one lashing has gone through two oblong, countersunk holes and probably another has been in a wide groove near the top. A characteristic feature of this specimen is the wide, deep, transversal cut in the upper part of the flat surface. The other specimen has been secured by a lashing over the lower part supported by a step and possibly through one or both the oblong holes.

Plate 26.1-9 are examples of wooden objects that occur in the find in considerable numbers and

---

[188] Murdoch 1892: figs. 426 and 428; Larsen 1934: 129-130.
[189] Mathiassen 1928: 155-156.
[190] Nelson 1899: fig. 21.

which, because they are all made of branches of willow and alder of approximately the same size, are considered to belong in the same category. There are two types, one cylindrical (Pl. 26.5-9) and one which is more or less triangular (Pl. 26.1-4). Of the former, there are 36 specimens ranging in length from 6.5 to 1.8 cm and in diameter from 4.0 cm (Pl. 26.6) to 1.0 cm. Most of them are circular in cross section and with carefully whittled ends; Pl. 26.9 probably shows a stage in the production of two. The second type comprises six specimens, which range in size from 6.2 x 3.7 cm (Pl. 26.3) to 4.4 x 2.4 cm. Their function is undetermined, if they indeed had the same function. They are all very light, hence an immediate interpretation of them would be as floats and they might be, but for what? Neither at Point Hope nor at Deering is there any sign of the use of fishhooks or nets, but could they perhaps have been used in connection with snares? The pronounced notch in the triangular form clearly shows that a line of some sort has been attached to it and they could be toggles, but it does not seem very likely that the cylindrical specimens have been used as such. For the time being I prefer the term *"floats"* for both types.

In the collection there are one almost complete and four fragmentary *round wooden discs*, which may or may not belong in the same category (Pl. 26.10-13). No. 11 could be half of a disk for a top, but of the others only no. 10 has a hole in the middle and as that is oblong and off center, it could hardly have served as a top. This almost complete specimen is 0.8 cm thick, somewhat thinner along the edge, and is reminiscent of a bottom of a container with baleen or wooden sides. However, this is probably not the explanation of this specimen, which besides the hole in the middle has the remnants of a 2 cm long extension. Of the two unidentifiable specimens, Pl. 26.12 and 13, the latter is interesting because of the ten mostly unfinished perforations along the edge. They are obviously not drilled but gouged out from both sides.

Plate 26.18 is one of four *awl-shaped wooden sticks* ranging in length from 12.0 to 7.3 cm. They might have been used like awls of antler or ivory. Plate. 26.16-17 are two *flat, wooden sticks with undulating edges*. Though slightly different, they seem to be examples of the same kind of object consisting of a short, round shaft and a longer blade with undulating edges. Distinctive features of no.16 are a groove around the top of the shaft and pair of notches near the base of the blade, and of no.17 a longitudinal rib on both sides of the blade. Their use is undetermined. The carefully carved wooden piece Pl. 26.19 is broken off a larger, unknown object.

Plate 27.1-2 is two of 6 wooden objects for which the use of which is undetermined. The two specimens, which are about the same size, are characterized by one flat and one rounded surface, the former furnished with a 1 cm wide, deep transverse groove near each end (Pl. 27.2), the latter with an incision for a lashing outside two wide grooves. They seem to have functioned as cross pieces lashed to two narrow, parallel (?) edges or mouldings, possibly like Pl. 27.3-5. Unless they are parts of boats, I have no suggestion regarding their function. The *mouldings* referred to above are three examples of a total of 37 pieces in the collection. Pl. 27.3 is the largest specimen; the others range in width from 1.0 to 1.5 cm. Characteristic of this type of artifact is one flat side, a semi lunar to triangular cross section, and notches, often oblique, in the rounded surface. These notches are probably meant for strings with which the moulding has been tied to another object. Pl. 27.5 shows a specimen with a long scarf-surface indicating that it has been made longer. Pl. 27.6-9 are three out of 17 wooden *sticks with marks of lashing*. No.6 has been bound with two narrow bands crossing each other. Nos. 7-9 are three of 9 specimens which may be parts of the same kind of artifact. Most are more or less curved, elliptical in cross section, and with a smooth surface. Five of them have had a scarf joint, like no. 7 in which the willow root lashing is preserved. They could have been parts of loops.

Plate 27.12 is one of three specimens which undoubtedly are parts of the same kind of artifact and which were found in the same layer of the house. They are all about the same size, flat on both sides, cut off at one end and with two notches and an oblong perforation at the other. Their function is undetermined. The two oblong, flat pieces of wood, Pl. 27.14-15, have two features in common, namely a pair of oblong perforations which on one side are connected with a deep groove and, on the same side, marks of friction against snow, both features characteristic of the sled runners described earlier. No. 14 is reworked and appears to be an unfinished fragment of a toy sled runner. The front part is made thinner by whittling. No. 15 is most likely a fragment of a sled runner, although the placing of the holes does not conform to that of the other runners, where the holes are in the front part. The present piece however is cut off as if it were the rear end of a runner.

Fifty-seven *wooden stakes* sharpened to a more or less battered point were found in and around the house, most of them inside the walls, 14 in the 3rd floor alone (Pl. 28.9-12). The longest specimen is 50 cm and the thickest, 4.0 cm in diameter. Most of them show signs of having been near fire. It is noteworthy that 10 of the longest specimens are mostly charred in a belt 20-40 cm above the point, while the lower part in most cases is untouched by the fire. In this connection it should be mentioned that many stakes and stakes holes were found around the fireplace, particularly in the 3rd floor (fig. 14). A few of the stakes are marked with incisions; Pl. 28.10-12 with an X, Pl. 28.9 with three parallel, oblique lines, one specimen with 6 short, parallel lines, and another specimen with 12 short, equally spaced lines.

Plate 28.13 is one out of 7 specimens that have been classified as *long, flat wooden sticks* which may have served the same, so far undetermined, function. The illustrated specimen is the most complete and best executed but four more are of about the same size and shape. In addition there are two with flat, rounded points.

Some of the most surprising artifacts in the collection are a number of *thin wooden boards*, which at the first glance seem to be made by means of a saw. Only careful examination of the surfaces in proper light reveals the marks of the tool, probably an adze, which has been used in the production. More astonishing is the fact that the thickness of each board does not vary more than 1-2 millimeter. Most are about 1 cm thick; the thickest is 1.8 cm. Several specimens are like Pl. 28.1-3, cut off at the ends as straight as if sawn but it has probably been done with a splitting knife. In both ends of Pl. 28.2 and in one end of Pl. 28.1 and 7 the cut has been made in two steps leaving a rabbet, the most likely explanation of which seems to be that these boards have been sides of boxes. If this is the case, which is by no means certain, the two

holes near each end of two of the specimens may have been made for lashings to keep two sides together. One could go still further and suggest that the holes along the long sides of nos.1 and 2 had served the same purpose. These two specimens are almost complete and three of the margins of Pl. 28.3 are intact. Twenty-nine specimens, some of them as large as 61 x 12 cm and 51.5 x 11 cm, have been classified as thin boards but only 13 of them could have been parts of boxes, if that interpretation is correct. Pl. 28.6, which is painted black on both sides, could have been, but Pl. 28.4 and 5 could not. The former is curved and has a rounded margin and the latter has obviously also served another, undetermined, purpose. One side of the latter shows the same kind of wear as on sled runners, the other side is partly covered with marks of a stone scraper.

Plate 28.8 is the only specimen of its kind in the collection. It is almost complete, 1.4 cm thick, has four oblong perforations, near one end one square hole is filled out with a wooden peg, and remains of a similar hole are at the other end. In both ends the margin has been roughened indicating that the object has been fastened at both ends, but so far its use is undetermined. A number of other wooden objects of undetermined use is represented by only one specimen. On the off chance that similar objects should turn up in other finds, some of them will be illustrated for comparison. Pl. 27.10 is part of a carefully made shaft with a large, rectangular perforation through its thickest part near one end and a smaller, oblong perforation at right angles to it further down the shaft. Pl. 27.11 is wedge-shaped with one flat side which is roughened with coarse transverse cuts meant for securing it to some other object. On the other, rounded side are six stops with incisions for lashings. Pl. 27.13 is part of a heavy willow root grown in a peculiar shape which undoubtedly has inspired someone to make five pairs of oblique and transverse incisions on one side and to tie a string of baleen below a knob (head?) in one end. This strange object may be a plaything, perhaps representing some animal or, maybe it was connected to the spiritual life of the people (?).

The wooden objects illustrated in Plate 29 are, with a few exceptions, unique and unidentified. No. 1 is a round, smooth stick with a conical point of each end and two round perforations. No. 2 has the appearance of a drill shaft but has probably served another purpose since, the assemblage contains no mouthpieces or drill bits, and since all holes seem to be gouged out. No. 3 is a handle, possibly for a beaver tooth knife. It is round, slightly curved and has a groove in one end. On the reverse side in the upper end are the remains of a schematic face, one eye, the mouth, and two horizontal cheek lines. No. 4 of willow or alder, may also be a handle for a beaver tooth knife (compare to Giddings 1964: Pl. 14.13). Characteristic of No. 5 are the staggered notches at the end of a round stick. No.6 is a small willow branch hollowed out and with a transverse groove near one end. It was possibly part of a snare similar to those of bird bone. No.7 is a flat piece of wood with a V-shaped incision in each end; No.8, a round piece of wood with a deep groove around the middle. No.9 is a fragment of a flat, 0.4 cm thick object with an oblong perforation. No. 10 is made of a piece of hard wood and has a very smooth surface. The longitudinal groove is 7 cm deep. No. 11 is a flat toggle-like object, 0.9 cm thick. Nos. 12 and 13, though not found together, are obviously part of the same object, probably a paddle. They are painted black on both sides and increase in thickness from the edge towards the middle, No.13 from 0.5 to 1.8 cm, No. 12 a little less. No.14 is paddle-shaped, completely flat on the reverse side and arched on the other. The very smooth surfaces show traces of a stone tool. No. 15 is two pieces of the same object one side of which is crosshatched. No.16 and one other similar piece have gouged out holes in the corners. No. 17 has the shape and other characteristics of a snowshoe crosspiece though in miniature and without holes.

Of the 42 *unidentified objects of antler*, 16 are illustrated in Plate 30. No. 1 is a flat, slightly curved object with a deep groove, in the bottom of which there are three oblong perforations. No. 2 is a piece similar in shape, but which has a longitudinal groove on each side extending from a oblong perforation. No.3 is also flat and slightly curved; it has an oblong perforation and a short, wide groove on one side. No.4 is very carefully made with a polished outer surface, which on the thin part has an inlay consisting of a plug of the same kind as used on the throwing stick in fig. 21. The reverse side is concave and it is obvious that the object has been made to fit a rounded surface and was probably fastened with plugs through the two holes. The thin part, which forms an extension, is curved and may have formed a hook but the end is broken off. Most likely it was attached to a weapon. Nos. 5 and 6 may be two examples of the same artifact. They both have a thicker upper part, rounded in cross section, while the lower part is flat. The thin, curved stick, no. 7, is pointed at both ends and has remnants of longitudinal lines. No. 8 has an unfinished appearance and may be an arrowhead blank. No. 9, which has a flat, smooth under side has been attached to some other object, probably of wood, and held in place with lashing across the flat extensions on each side of the central hole. It is reminiscent of a drill mouthpiece but the hole is elliptic and has no sign of wear. The ends show marks of a beaver tooth tool. No. 10 is one of two rings cut out of antler without further work done to them. In no. 11, a piece of antler been hollowed out to form a ladle-like object with smooth edges. The curved shaft, no. 12, is elliptic in cross section and flat with sharp edges at both ends. Possibly it is a blank of a salmon spear prong. No. 13 is a dagger like implement of a hollowed out piece of antler having a definite "handle" with rounded edges. No.14 is a flat, curved piece of antler, which is slightly concave on one side and has two oblong perforations connected with a wide groove. No. 15 is reminiscent of the arrowheads of fantastic forms (Type 7) from Point Hope. The specimen in question is elliptic in cross section and has an unfinished tang. The small projection at the other end is completely split in two and the cut proceeds in a longitudinal line. Finally, no. 16 seems to be a blank of a barbed prong, the point of which has been reworked.

IV. References

Adney, Edwin T. & Howard I. Chapelle
1964: The Bark Canoes and Skin Boats of North America. Smithsonian Institution, U.S. National Museum, Bulletin no. 230. Washington D.C.

Allen, Henry T.
1887: Report of an Expedition to the Copper, Tanana, and Kouyukon Rivers, in the Territory of Alaska, in the Year 1885. Washington: U.S. Government Printing Office.

Arima, Eugene Y.
1963: Report on an Eskimo Umiak Build at Ivujivik, P. Q. in the Summer of 1960. Anthropological Series 59. National Museum of Canada Bulletin. Ottawa.

1975: A Contextual Study of the Caribou Eskimo Kayak. National Museum of Man, Mercury Series. Canadian Ethnology Notes on the Kayak and its Equipment at Inuyivik, P. Q. National Museum of Canada, Bulletin No. 194. Contributions to Anthropology, 1961-62, pt. II:221-261. Ottawa.

Arnold J.R. & Libby, W.F.
1951: Radiocarbon Dates. Science 113:111-120.

Berg, Gösta
1935: Sledges and Wheeled Vehicles. Nordiska Museets Handlingar; 4, Stockholm and Copenhagen.

Birket-Smith, Kaj
1929: The Caribou Eskimos. Material and social life and their cultural position. Report of the fifth Thule Expedition, 1921-24. The Danish expedition to Arctic North America in charge of Knud Rasmussen, Copenhagen, vol. 5.

1945: Ethnographical Collections from the Northwest Passage. Report of the fifth Thule Expedition, 1921-24. The Danish expedition to Arctic North America in charge of Knud Rasmussen, Copenhagen, vol. 6.

Bogoras, Waldemar
1904-09: The Chukchee. Memoirs of the American Museum of National History, vol. 11.

Campbell
1959: The Kayuk Complex of Arctic Alaska. American Antiquity 25(1):94-105. Salt Lake City.

Cantwell, John C.
1887: A Narrative account of the exploration of Kowak River, Alaska, under the direction of Capt. Michael A. Healey. In: Healey, M.A., Report of the cruise of the revenue marine steamer "Corwin" in the Arctic Ocean in the year 1885. Washington.

1889: A Narrative Account of the Exploration of the Kowak River, Alaska. In Report of the Cruise of the Revenue Marine Steamer Corwin in the Arctic Ocean in the Year 1884, by Capt. M.A. Healy U.S.R.M. Washington: U.S. Government Printing Office.

Clark, Donald W.
1977: Hahunadan Lake: An Ipiutak-Related Occupation of Western Interior Alaska. Archaeological Survey of Canada, Paper No. 71, Mercury Series, National Museum of Man. Ottawa.

Clark, Donald W. & Anette M. Clark
1974: Koyukon Athapaskan houses as seen through oral tradition and through archaeology. Arctic Anthropology 11, supplement.

Collins, Henry B.
1937: Archaeology of St. Lawrence Island, Alaska. Smithsonian Misc. Coll., vol. 96(1).

Davidson, David S.
1937: Snowshoes. Memoirs of the American Philosophical Society, vol. 6. Philadelphia.

Ford, James A.
1959: Eskimo Prehistory in the Vicinity of Point Barrow, Alaska. Anthropological Papers of the American Museum of National History 47(1). New York.

Geist Otto W.& Rainey, Froelich G.
1936: Archaeological Excavations at Kukulik, St. Lawrence Island, Alaska. Misc. Publikations of University of Alaska, vol. 2. Washington

Giddings, Louis J.
1952: The Arctic Woodland Culture of the Kobuk River. Museum Monographs. Philadelphia.

1961: Kobuk River People. University of Alaska Studies of Northern Peoples No. 1. College.

1964: The Archaeology of Cape Denbigh. Providence: Brown University Press.

1967: Ancient Men of the Arctic. New York: Knopf.

Giddings, Louis J. & Douglas D. Anderson
1986: Beach Ridge Archaeology of Cape Krusenstern. Publications in Archaeology 20, National Park Service, U.S. Department of the Interior. Washington D.C.

Hatt, Gudmund
1916: Kyst- og indlandskultur i det arktiske. Geografisk Tidskrift 23:284-290.

Holtved, Erik
1944: Archaeological investigations in the Thule district. Meddelelser om Grønland vol. 141(1&2), Copenhagen.

Honigman, John J.
1954: The Kaska Indians: An Ethnographic Reconstruction. Yale University Publications in Anthropology, vol. 51:5-163. New Haven.

Hough, Walter
1892: The Bernadon, Allen and Jony Korean Collections in the U. S. National Museum. Reports of the U.S. National Museums Annual Report of the Smithsonian Institute 1891, Sec. III:429-488. Washington.

Jenness, Diamond
1932: The Indians of Canada. National Museum of Canada. Bulletin 65 Anthropological Series No. 15. Ottawa.
1960: The Indians of Canada. Bulletin of the National Museum of Canada, No. 65. 5th edition. Ottawa.

Jones, Strachan
1867: Notes on the Tinnek or Chepewyan Indians of British and Russian America. 3. The Kutchin Tribes. Annual Report of the Smithsonian Institution:320-327.

Laguna, Frederica de
1947: The Prehistory of Northern North America as seen from the Yukon. Memoirs of the Society of American Archaeology, No. 3

Larsen, Helge
1934: Dødemandsbugten, an Eskimo settlement on Clavering Island. Meddelelser om Grønland, vol. 102(1). Copenhagen.
1950: Archaeological Investigations in Southwestern Alaska. American Antiquity 15(3):177-186. Salt Lake City.
1958: The Material Culture of the Nunamiut and its Relation to other forms of Eskimo Culture in Northern Alaska. Proceedings from the 32nd International Congress of Americanists. Copenhagen.
1968: Trail Creek: Final Report on the Excavation of Two Caves on Seward Peninsula Alaska. Acta Arctica 15. Copenhagen.

Larsen, Helge & Meldgaard, Jørgen
1958: Paleo-Eskimo Cultures in Disko Bugt, West Greenland. Meddelelser om Grønland 161(2). Copenhagen.

Larsen, Helge & Rainey, Froelich G.
1948: Ipiutak and the Arctic Whale Hunting Culture. Anthropological Papers of the American Museum of Natural History 42. New York.

Levin, M.G. & Potapov, L. P.
1964: The Peoples of Siberia. Stephen Dunn, translation editor. Chicago and London. University of Chicago Press.

Mason, Otis T.
1896: Primitive Travel and Transportation. Report of the U.S. National Museum for 1894. Washington D.C.
1904: Aboriginal American basketry: Studies in a Textile Art Nithout Machinery. Report of the U.S. National Museum. Annual Report of the Smithsonian Institution 1902. Washington.

Mason, A. J.
1946: Notes on the Indians of the Great Slave Lake Area. Yale University Publications in Anthropology, Nos. 33 & 34. No. 34:1-46.

Mathiassen, Therkel
1928: Material culture of the Iglulik Eskimos. Report of the fifth Thule Expedition, 1921-24. The Danish expedition to Arctic North America in charge of Knud Rasmussen, Copenhagen, vol. 6(1):1-249
1931: Ancient Eskimo Settlements in the Kangâmiut Area. Meddelelser om Grønland 91(1). Kommisionen for Videnskabelige Undersøgelser. Copenhagn.

McKennan,
1959: The Upper Tanana Indians. Yale University Publications in Anthropology, No. 7. New Haven.

Murdoch, John
1885: Natural History, pp. 89-200 in Report of the International Expedition to Point Barrow Alaska. Pt. 4. Washington: U. Ss. Government Printing Office.
1892: Ethnological Results of the Point Barrow Expedition. In: 9th Annual Report of the Bureau of American Ethnology for the Years 1887-1888:19-441. Washington D.C.

Nelson, Edward W.
1899: The Eskimo About Bering Strait. In: 18th Annual Report of the Bureau of American Ethnology for the Years 1896-1897:3-518. Washington D.C.

Osgood, Cornelius
1932: The Ethnography of the Great Bear Lake Indians. National Museum of Canada Annual Report for 1931. Bulletin No. 70:31-98. Ottawa.
1936: The Distribution of Northern Athapaskan Indians. Yale University Publications in Anthropology, No. 7:1-23. New Haven.
1937: The ethnography of the Tanaina. Yale University Publications in Anthropology, no. 16. New Haven
1940: Ingalik Material Culture. Yale University Publications in Anthropology, No. 22: 500 pages. New Haven
1971: The Han Indians: A compilation of ethnographic and historical data on the Alaska-Yukon boundary area. Yale University Publications in Anthropology, No. 74. New Haven.

Oswalt, Wendell, H.
1952: The Archaeology of Hooper Bay Village, Alaska. Anthropological Papers of the University of Alaska 1(1):47-91. Fairbanks.

Rainey, Froelich G.

1941: The Ipiutak Culture at Point Hope, Alaska. American Anthropology, new series, vol. 43:364-374.

Rasmussen, Knud

1932: Intellectual Culture of the Copper Eskimos. Report of the fifth Thule Expedition, 1921-24. The Danish expedition to Arctic North America, Copenhagen, vol. 9.

Rudenko, S.I.

1961: The Ancient Culture of the Bewring Sea and the Eskimo Problem. Arctic Institute of North America, Anthropology of the North: Translations from Russian Sources No. 1 (edi. Michaeil, Henry N.). University of Toronto Press. Toronto.

Schrenck, P.L. von

1881: Reisen und Forschungen in Amur-Lande in den Jahren 1854-1856. St. Petersburg, Kaiserliche Akademie der Wissenschaften, vol. 3.

Tauber, Henrik

1962: Copenhagen Radiocarbon Dates V, part II(a), Alaska. Radiocarbon 4:29.

Taylor, William E.

1968: The Arnapik and Tyara Sites: An Archaeological Study of Dorset Culture Origins. Memoir for the Society for American Archaeology, No. 22. Salt Lake City.

VanStone, James W. & Charlie V. Lucier

1974: An early archaeological example of tattoing from Northwest Alaska. Fieldiana anthropology 66(1):9 pages. Field Museum of Natural History.

Woldt, A.

1884: Capitain Jacobsen's Reise an der Nordwestküste Amerikas 1881-1883. Zum zwecke ethnologischer Sammlungen und Erkundigungen nebst Beschreibung persönlicher Erlebnisse für den deutschen Leserkreis bearbeitet. Leipzig 1884: 432 pages.

Appendix A

FAUNAL REMAINS

All animal bones, most of them fragmentary, were collected from the 1st and 2nd floor of the main room. With his usual willingness and acknowledged expertise Dr. Ulrik Møhl of the Zoological Museum of Copenhagen examined the material which resulted in a report that forms the basis for this chapter. The material, consisting of 686 identifiable pieces, is divided up into marine and terrestrial game which were distributed as follows:

Marine Game	1st floor	2nd floor
Ringed Seal (*Phoca hispida*)	200	130
Bearded Seal (*Erignathus barbatus*)	35	45
Common (Spotted) Seal (*Phoca vitulina*)	8	6
Walrus (*Odobenus rosmarus*)	7	3
Whales (*Cetacea sp.*)	1	7
Thick-billed Murre (*Uria lomvia*)	60	8
Total (marine)	**311**	**199**

Terrestrial Game	1st floor	2nd floor
Caribou (*Rangifer articus*)	60	60
Snowshoe Hare (*Lepus americanus*)	2	-
Fox (*Vulps fulva*)	1	2
Wolf (*Canis lupus*)	2	-
Beaver (*Castor canadensis*)	-	1
Geese sp. (*Anser sp.*)	30	16
Whistling Swan (*Olor columbianus*)	-	1
Willow Ptarmigan (*Lagopus lagopus*)	1	-
Total (terrestrial)	**96**	**80**

It is worth noting that there is a surprising agreement between the figures of the two floor layers, which indicates that the fauna and the hunting conditions have been the same in the two periods of occupation. Also noticeable is the fact that, according to the figures, almost three times as much of the game was caught in the sea as on land. The most important is the ringed seal with almost half of all the bones. This, the most common of all arctic sea mammals, is present in northwestern Alaska all year round but most numerous when and where there is sea ice. Consequently, almost all seal hunting takes place from October-November when the ice begins to form until July when it disappears. Another seal, which occurs and is hunted at the same time, is the bearded seal. It is just as important as the ringed seal

because, although the bones found in the house numerically make up only 11.5% of the total, not only is it about double the size of the ringed seal but its thick skin is essential for many purposes, for example as lines and boat covers.

Two other species of marine mammals are represented, the common seal and walrus, but judging from the number of bones they are of minor importance in comparison with the ringed seal and the bearded seal. The common seal (also called spotted seal or harbour seal) seldom occurs on or around sea ice so the specimens here were probably caught in the summer or early fall. Though walrus often occurs around sea ice, the hunting in these waters usually takes place in the summer. It was probably hunted as much its valuable tusks as for its meat. The few pieces of whalebone were too small to be identified to species. White whales may have been hunted, but bones of the larger whales probably come from stranded whales. The presence of bird-cliffs at Cape Deceit account for the many bones of thick-billed murre. It is noticeable that most of the larger bones, particularly the humeri, are broken in order to get the nutritious, fatty marrow. The presence of these bird bones is another indication of summer hunting.

The only fish bones found were two vertebrae of salmon species. This is surprising, given the abundance of salmon in the water outside Deering in August 1950. Considering the exceptionally good state of preservation of organic materials it is inconceivable that not more bones should have been preserved if salmon had been consumed in the house in any quantity. That the occupants have utilized this excellent and easily accessible source of food is obvious from the presence in the assemblage of a relatively large number of salmon spear parts. The only explanation seems to be that they must have prepared and eaten the fish somewhere else.

As may be expected, caribou is by far the most important land game. Not only is caribou meat highly valued by all arctic peoples but in addition the caribou is an important source of skin for clothing, bedding and tents, antler and bone for weapons and tools, and sinew for sewing. There are bones from all parts of the animal showing that whole animals were brought back to the house, which again shows that the hunting had taken place not too far away. All limb bones were broken in order to get at the marrow. Also the lower parts of the jawbones are broken, in this case to obtain the fat that surrounds the nerves in canalis mandibularis. Judging from the size of the bones, the caribou we are dealing with must have been very large. As an example it may be mentioned that the upper ends of two metacarpi measure 41 mm transversally and 31 mm anteriorly-posterily in comparison with 31 mm and 28 mm as maximum measurements on the same bone of six, recent adult bucks from West Greenland. This means that conditions for caribou at that time must have been very favourable.

The number of bones of other land mammals is too small to draw any conclusions from their presence except that they were hunted, the wolves and foxes probably mainly for their skin, and hare for their food value. In addition to the beaver in the list the find comprises several beaver incisors used as tools.

Of the land game geese seem to have played an important role. The bones are too fragmentary to identify species, but according to the present distribution they may be from snow geese, white-fronted geese, or Canada geese. All are migratory so they must have been taken in the summer. Because all the bones seem to belong to adult birds it is most likely that they were taken in the last part of July when they moult their flight feathers and are unable to fly. During that period they gather in large flocks and graze in meadows where they are easily caught by hand or killed with a stick. At Deering they could have been taken on the flats just back of the house.

In addition to the bones mentioned above the find contains two skulls of adult dogs and an almost complete skeleton of a pup. The dogs are very similar to the rather large, strongly built Eskimo type of dogs, as known from Alaska through Canada to Greenland.

Though the number of bones found in the two floor layers is rather small, they do give us some information about the time of occupation of the house and the sustenance of its occupants. The presence of bones of migratory birds like thick-billed murre, geese and swans are sure evidence of summer activity and the spotted seal was probably also taken in the summer. All of them are, however, of minor importance compared to ringed seal, bearded seal, and caribou, which form the foundation for an existence in this part of the world. However, they do not tell us much about the period of occupation of the house. Caribou at least were probably available all the year round and the other two at least from October-November till July, which means that as far as the bones are concerned, the house could have been occupied during the whole year or any part of it.

Appendix B

DATING

Deering was among the very first archaeological sites to be dated by the radiocarbon method. A piece of wood from the third floor-layer of the house had been submitted to the dating laboratory in Chicago by Dr. Froelich G. Rainey, who in 1948 had become a member of "The Committee on Carbon 14 of the American Anthropological Association and the Geological Society of America". In the first published list of radiocarbon dates from 1950, the Deering sample appears as number 260 and is dated at 973 + 170 years old. The next number on the same list (no. 266) is also a sample of Ipiutak culture, namely a piece of wood from Burial 51 at Point Hope, and the date of this is given as 912 + 179 years old.[1] The dates were surprising and undeniably disappointing to Rainey and me, because even if the two dates are almost identical we could not accept them as valid. In the first place they were much younger than our estimated age for the Ipiutak culture at Point Hope[2] and, secondly, they were too young in comparison with other forms of Eskimo culture in the same general area. As we shall see presently the first Ipiutak ^{14}C dates were actually 300-400 years too young, which may be connected with the fact that the first measurements were made on solid carbon and not as later on CO_2.

In 1962 two samples from Deering were submitted to radiocarbon dating at the laboratory at Copenhagen. One sample, a piece of birch bark, from section B-13 outside the house was dated at 1380 + 200 BP, and the other sample, K-537, consisting of dog faeces from the Anteroom, at 1290 + 200 BP.[3]

In 1976 the Copenhagen laboratory dated five samples from the house, one from each of the five floor layers. The samples were all of wood, and the results were as follows:

Except for the date of the third floor, the dates form a chronological sequence covering about 100 years, which should give us the approximate duration of the occupation of the house. The only

Sample No.	Floor-layer No.	Years BP
K-2605	1	1180 + 55
K-2605	1	1220 + 75
Average K-2605	1	1190 + 45
K-2606	2	1240 + 75
K-2607	3	1440 + 75
K-2607	3	1370 + 75
Average K-2607	3	1400 + 55
K-2608	4	1250 + 75
K-2609	5	1290 + 75
K-2609	5	1340 + 75
Average K-2609	5	1320 + 55

explanation for the aberrant date of the third floor seems to be that the sample was of an older piece of wood, which for some reason was present in that layer.

The natural consequence of the latest dating of the Deering samples was to try to get some new ^{14}C dates from the Ipiutak site at Point Hope. Until 1976 we only had two dates from Point Hope, the Chicago date from 1950 and a date of some arrowheads of antler measured by the University of Pennsylvania C-14 Laboratory in 1958. This sample (P-98) appeared to be 1619 ± 210 BP.

For comparison with Deering, samples from five Point Hope Ipiutak houses were selected for dating at the Copenhagen laboratory. As far as possible the houses chosen were situated at different parts of the very extensive site. The samples were:

Sample No.	House No.	Material	Years BP
K-2742	3	Wooden stick	1300 + 70
K-2743	32	Worked antler	1320 + 70
K-2744	43	Worked antler	1210 + 70
K-2744	43	Worked antler	1380 + 70
Average K-2744	43	Worked antler	1290 + 70
K-2745	45	Antler wedge	1490 + 70
K-2746	69	Wooden sledge runner	1390 + 70

Considering the length of time it must have taken to built up a site as large as Ipiutak, it is surprising that the dates do not show greater variation, actually three of the five are contemporary and contemporary with the first occupation of the Deering house. If we accept the datings from 1976, and I see no reason for not doing so, the main occupation of the Deering house is slightly younger than the Ipiutak manifestations at Point Hope.

---

[1] Arnold and Libby 1951s: 12.
[2] Ipiutak: 160.
[3] Tauber 1962: 29.

Appendix C

DISTRIBUTION OF SPECIMENS (ALL NUMBERS BEGINNING WITH P)

7051-7152	Main Room	1. floor
7153-7266	Main Room	2. floor
7267-7390C	Main Room	3. floor
7391-7524	Main Room	4. floor
7525-7649	Main Room	5. floor
7650-7704	Main Room	6. layer
7705-7789	Anteroom	1. layer
7790-7838	Anteroom	2. layer
7839-7894	Anteroom	3. layer
7895-7925	Anteroom	4. layer
7926-7969	Anteroom	5. layer
7970-8026	Anteroom	6. layer

8027-8045	between logs in west wall
8046-8060	below east wall
8061-8072	below logs in SW corner
8073-8114	outside walls, 1-30cm deep
8115-8131	outside walls

8132-8334	Field A
8335-8734	Field B

8735-8738	House without specific location
8739-8741	outside north wall
8742-8746	testdiggings

PLATE 1 (3:4)

1.	Arrow head – type 1	7839
2.	Arrow head – type 2	7525
3.	Arrow head – type 3	8550
4.	Arrow head – type 3	8426
5.	Arrow head – type 3	7061
6.	Arrow head – type 8	7393
7.	Bow fragment	7873
8.	Toy bow	8284
9.	Toy bow	8115
10.	Blunt arrow head (?)	7976
11.	Blunt arrow head (?)	7710
12.	Blunt arrow head (?)	8179
13.	Blunt arrow head (?)	8116
14.	Toy arrow shaft	7842
15.	Bow guard	7896
16.	Bow guard	7537
17.	Bow guard	8502

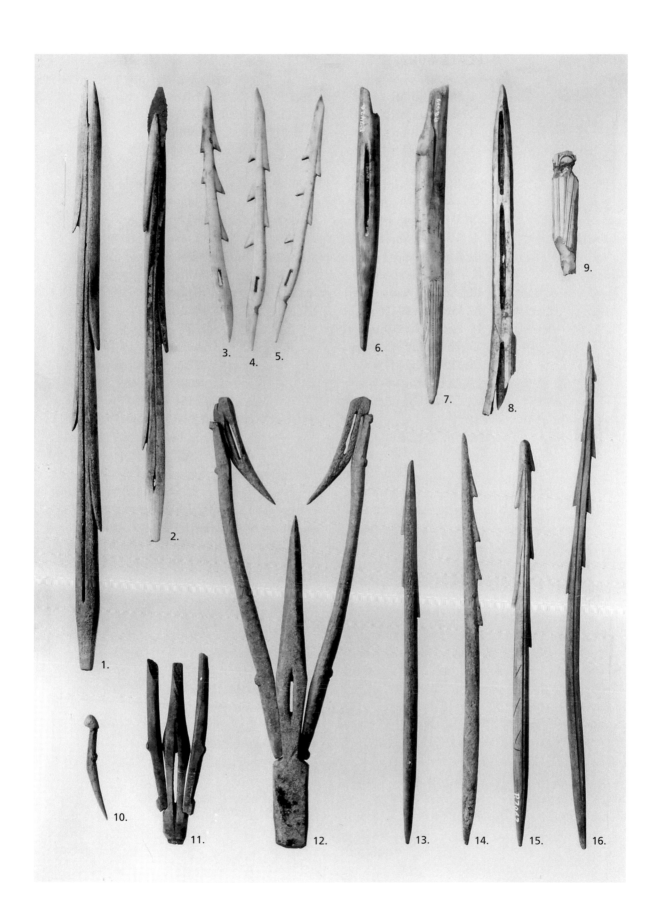

1. 2. 3. 4. 5. 6. 7. 8. 9. 10. 11. 12. 13. 14. 15. 16.

PLATE 4 (1:2)

1.	Shaft for bird dart	8501
2.	Shaft for bird dart	7217A
3.	Shaft for bird dart	7897
4.	Shaft for bird dart	7295
5.	Shaft for bird dart	7293
6.	Shaft for bird dart	8366
7.	Weapon shaft	7544
8.	Weapon shaft	8617
9.	Weapon shaft	7296
10.	Lance shaft ?	8428
11.	Harpoon shaft ?	7412
12.	Arrow (?) shaft with red paint	7542
13.	Weapon shaft	8444
14.	Arrow straightener (?)	7131
15.	Throwing stick	7425
16.	Throwing stick	7722
17.	Throwing stick	8664
1.	Throwing stick	8215

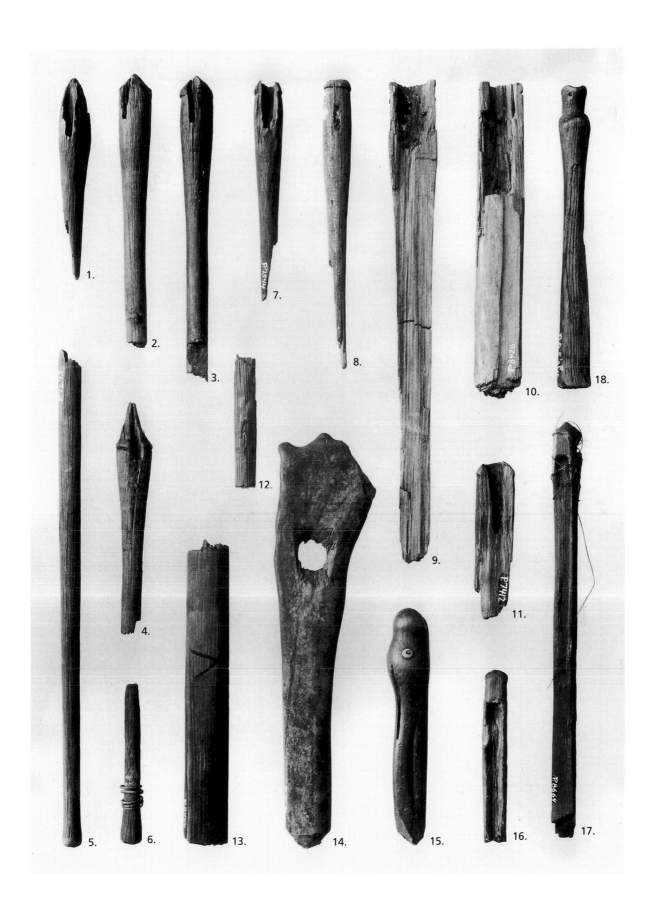

PLATE 5 (1:3)

1.	Sled runner fragment	8073
2.	Sled runner fragment	7756
3.	Sled runner fragment	8524
4.	Sled runner fragment	7287
5.	Sled runner fragment	7286
6.	Sled runner fragment	8646
7.	Sled runner fragment	7123
8.	Sled runner fragment	8038
9.	Toy sled runner	7505
10.	Toy sled runner	?
11.	Toy sled runner	7805
12.	Toy sled runner	7233

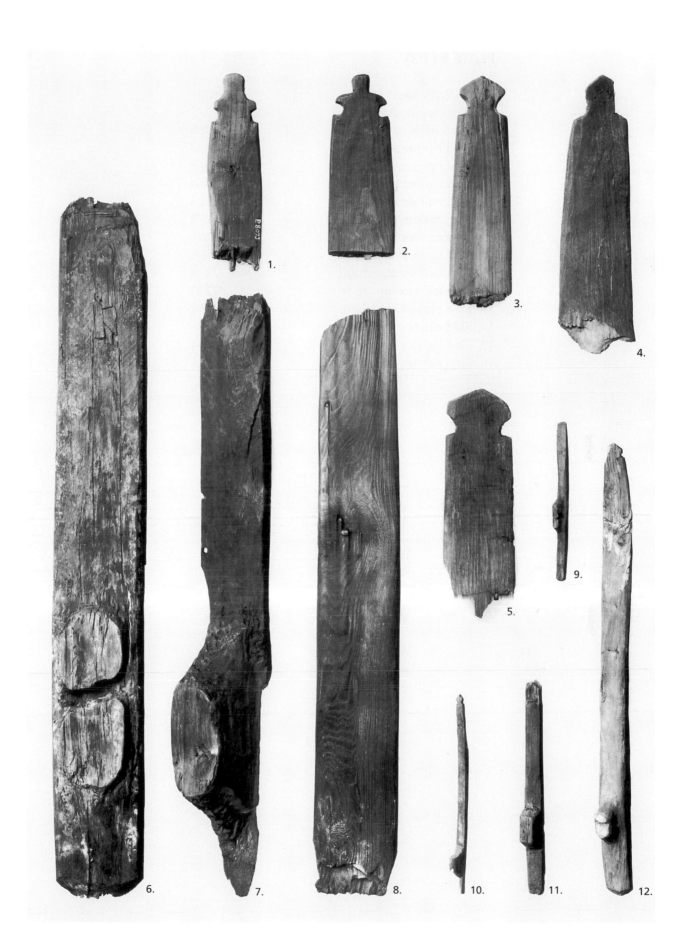

PLATE 6 (1:3)

1.	Arch for sled	8511
2.	Arch for sled	?
3.	Arch for sled	8060
4.	Sled runner stanchion	7765
5.	Sled runner stanchion	8163
6.	Sled runner stanchion	7364
7.	Sled runner stanchion	7126
8.	Sled runner stanchion	8607
9.	Sled runner stanchion	8436
10.	Sled runner stanchion	7126A
11.	Sled runner stanchion	7124
12.	Sled runner stanchion	7763
13.	Sled runner stanchion	7362
14.	Sled runner stanchion	7236
15.	Sled runner stanchion	7764
16.	Sled runner stanchion	7125

PLATE 7 (1:3)

1.	Snowshoe frame piece	8310
2.	Snowshoe frame piece	8160
3.	Snowshoe frame piece	8726
4.	Snowshoe frame piece	?
5.	Snowshoe frame piece	8052
6.	Snowshoe frame piece	8009
7.	Snowshoe cross piece	7360
8.	Snowshoe cross piece	8376
9.	Snowshoe cross piece	8008
10.	Snowshoe cross piece	7358
11.	Snowshoe cross piece	8007
12.	Snowshoe cross piece	7631
13.	Snowshoe cross piece	7359
14.	Snowshoe cross piece	8006
15.	Snowshoe cross piece	8435
16.	Snowshoe cross piece	7234
17.	Snowshoe cross piece	8386

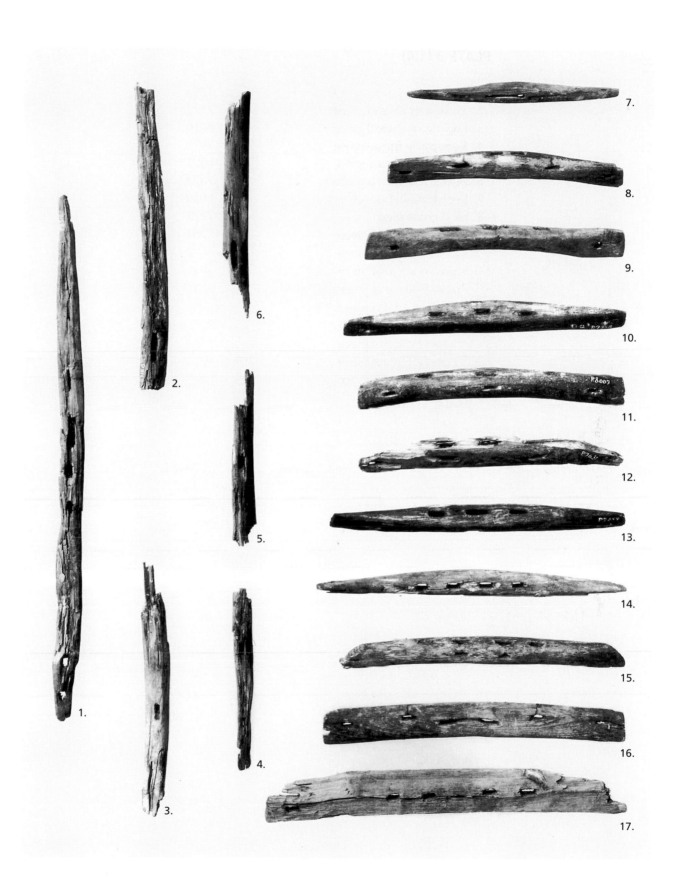

PLATE 8 (1:4)

1.	Paddle	7235
2.	Paddle or shovel	7122
3.	Paddle or shovel	8010
4.	Bow piece for canoe?	8477
5.	Bow piece for canoe?	8391
6.	Bow piece for canoe?	7874
7.	Sealskin boat cover	8019
8.	Sled cross piece?	7127
9.	Snowshoe frame piece	7357

1.

2.

3.

4.

5.

6.

7.

8.

9.

PLATE 9 (1:2)

1. Knife handle with side blade   7434
2. Knife handle for side blade   7724
3. Knife handle with side blade   8030
4. Knife handle for side blade   8463
5. Knife handle for side blade   8593
6. Knife handle for a single side blade   7725
7. Knife handle fragment   7726
8. Knife handle with side blade   7568
9. Knife handle for side blade   8622
10. Knife handle with side blade   8029
11. Knife handle for side blade   8670
12. Knife handle for side blade   8254

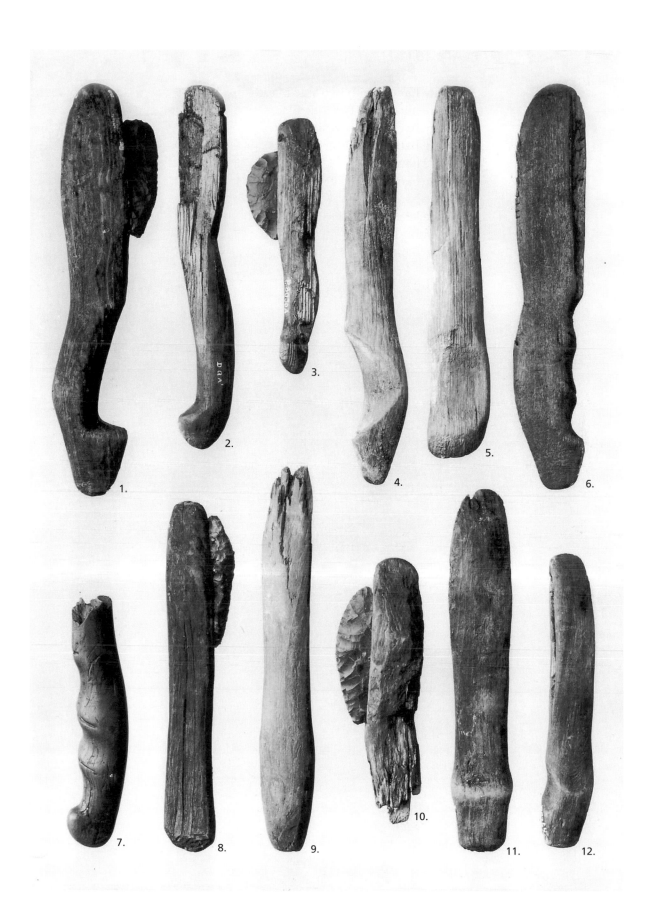

PLATE 10 (1:2)

1. Knife handle with two side blades   7979
2. Knife handle for two side blades   8241
3. Knife handle for two side blades   7723
4. Knife handle (for beaver tooth?)   7369
5. Adze handle   7311
6. Adze handle   7932
7. Adze handle   8355
8. Adze head with stone blade   7178
9. Toy adze handle   7438
10. Adze handle   8357

PLATE 11 (3:5)

1.	Knife handle for end blade, antler	8063
2.	Knife handle for end blade, antler	8209
3.	Knife handle for end blade, antler	7931
4.	Handle for splitting knife, antler	8716
5.	Handle for splitting knife, antler	8483
6.	Handle for splitting knife, antler	7075
7.	Handle for splitting knife, antler	8138
8.	Handle for splitting knife, antler	8210
9.	Handle for splitting knife, ivory	8292A
10.	Handle for splitting knife, antler	8354
11.	Handle for splitting knife, antler	7074
12.	Handle for splitting knife, antler	7307
13.	Handle for splitting knife, antler	7933
14.	Handle for splitting knife, antler	7564
15.	Handle for splitting knife, antler	8082
16.	Handle for splitting knife, antler	7930
17.	Beaver incisor	8364
18.	Flake tool, wooden shaft	7567A
19.	19. Flake tool, wooden shaft	7566B

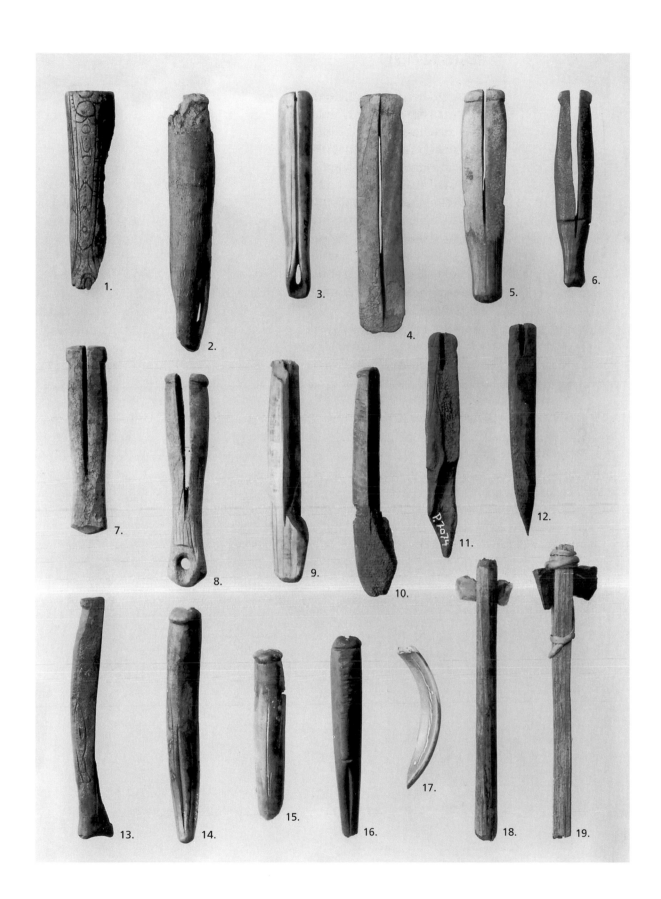

PLATE 12 (1:2)

1. Adze head – type 1, antler   7934
2. Adze head – type 1, antler   7308
3. Adze head – type 1, antler   8624
4. Adze head – type 1, antler   8674
5. Adze head – type 1, antler   7437
6. Adze head – type 1, antler   8623
7. Adze head – type 1, antler   7569A-B
8. Adze head – type 1, antler   8625
9. Adze head – type 1, antler   8293
10. Adze head – type 1, antler   7899
11. Adze head – type 2, bone   8595
12. Adze head – type 2, antler   7310
13. Adze head – type 2, bone   7308A
14. Adze blade, silicified slate   7078
15. Adze blade, silicified slate   8034
16. Adze blade, silicified slate   7986
17. 1Adze blade, silicified slate   7760

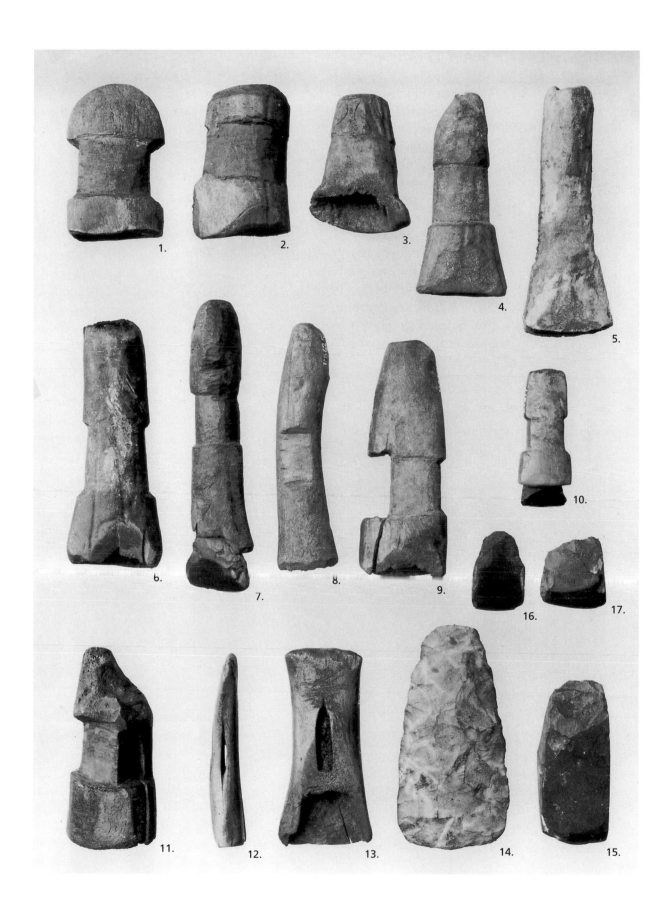

2. 3. 4. 5. 6. 7. 8. 9. 10. 11. 12. 13. 14. 15. 16. 17.

PLATE 13 (3:5)

1.	Flaker handle, antler	8739
2.	Flaker handle, antler	7312
3.	Hammer head, antler	7082
4.	Flaker point, bone	7443
5.	Flaker point, bone	7313
6.	Flaker point, bone	8401
7.	Flaker point, bone	7584
8.	Flaker point, bone	7583
9.	Flaker point, bone	8199
10.	Engraving tool, ivory	7076
11.	Two – hand scraper, bone	?
12.	Two – hand scraper, bone	?
13.	Scapula scraper, bone	?
14.	Scapula scraper, bone	?
15.	Cutting board, wood	?

1.
2.
3.
4.
5.
6.
7.
8.
9.
10.
11.
12.
13.
14.
15.

PLATE 14 (3:4)

1.	Side blade – type 2	8151
2.	Side blade – type 2	7730
3.	Side blade – type 1	7316
4.	Side blade – type 1	7090
5.	Side blade – type 1	8451
6.	Semi – lunar blade or blank	8087
7.	Semi – lunar blade or blank	7854
8.	Arrow point (?)	7315A
9.	Arrow point (?)	7909
10.	Insert blade – type 1	8086
11.	Insert blade – type 1	8404
12.	Insert blade – type 3	7449
13.	Discoidal blade – type 1	8632
14.	Discoidal blade – type 1	7458
15.	Discoidal blade – type 1	7595
16.	Discoidal blade – type 1	7459
17.	Discoidal blade – type 3	7983
18.	Discoidal blade – type 4	7193
19.	Discoidal blade – type 4	8676
20.	Discoidal blade – type 4	8741
21.	Discoidal blade – type 4	8720
22.	Discoidal blade – type 4	7097
23.	Discoidal blade – type 4	7461
24.	Discoidal blade – type 4	7096A

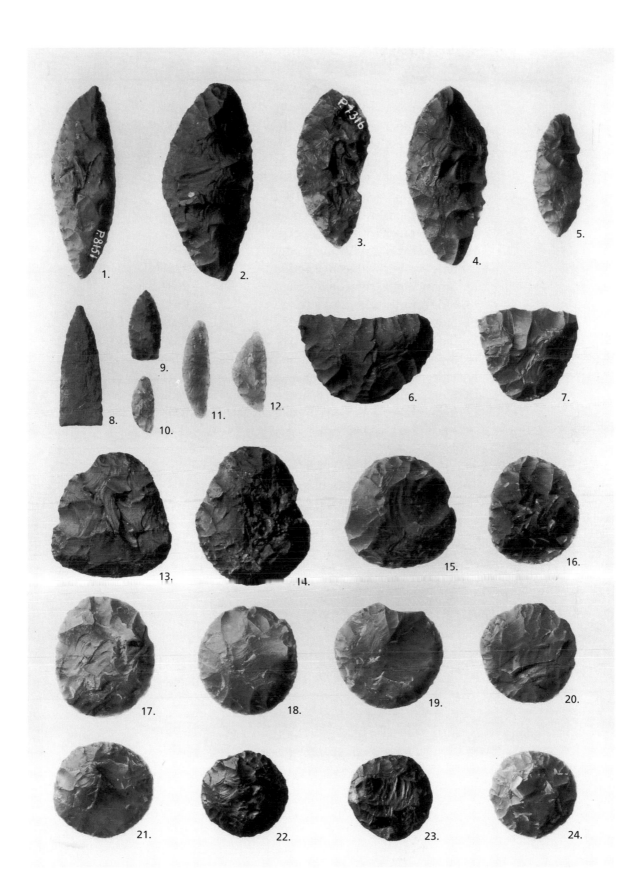

PLATE 15 (3:4)

1. Side scraper with concave edge   7466
2. Side scraper with concave edge   8678
3. Side scraper with concave edge   7460
4. Side scraper with concave edge   8677
5. Side scraper with concave edge   7198
6. Side scraper with straight edge   8457
7. Side scraper with straight edge   7735
8. Side scraper with straight edge   7734
9. Side scraper with straight edge   7472
10. Side scraper with straight edge   7939
11. Side scraper with convex edge   7201
12. Side scraper with convex edge   7602
13. Side scraper with convex edge   7987
14. Side scraper with convex edge   7609
15. Side scraper with two concave edges   8367
16. Side scraper with two concave edges   7463
17. Side scraper with two concave edges   7941
18. Side scraper with two concave edges   7605+7607
19. Side scraper with two concave edges   8455

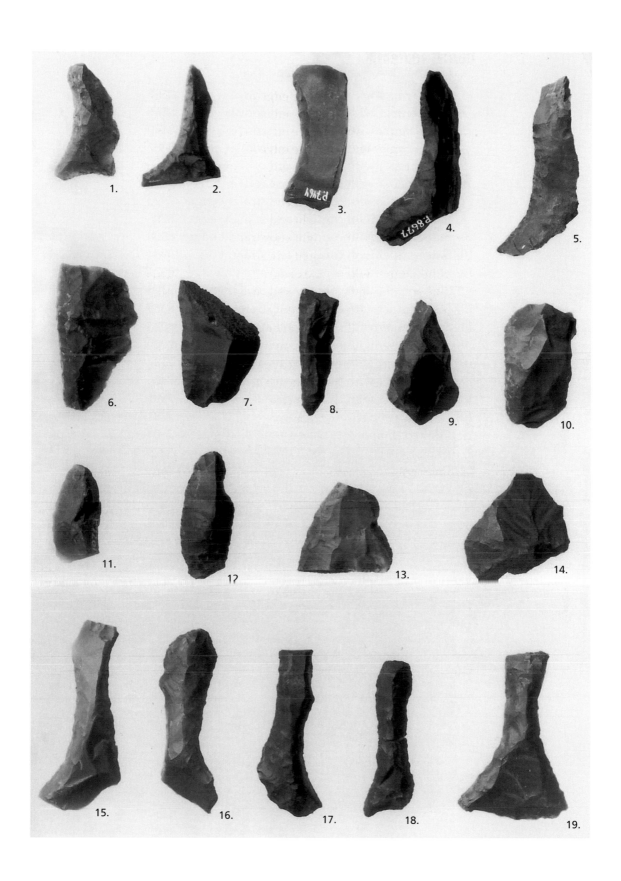

PLATE 16 (3:4)

1. Side scraper with concave and convex edge   7597
2. Side scraper with concave and convex edge   8566
3. Side scraper with concave and convex edge   8190
4. Side scraper with concave and convex edge   8407
5. Side scraper with concave and convex edge   8456
6. Side scraper with concave and convex edge   7194
7. Side scraper with concave and straight edge   7320
8. Side scraper with concave and straight edge   8298
9. Side scraper with concave and straight edge   8368
10. Side scraper with concave and straight dge   7984
11. Side scraper with concave and straight edge   7321
12. Side scraper with concave and straight edge   7195
13. Side scraper with convex and straight edge   8369
14. Side scraper with convex and straight edge   8035
15. Side scraper with two straight edges   7940
16. Side scraper with two straight edges   7197
17. Side scraper with two straight edges   7465
18. Side scraper with two straight edges   7195
19. Pointed scraper   7731
20. Pointed scraper   7604
21. End scraper   8279
22. End scraper   8635
23. Graver   7666

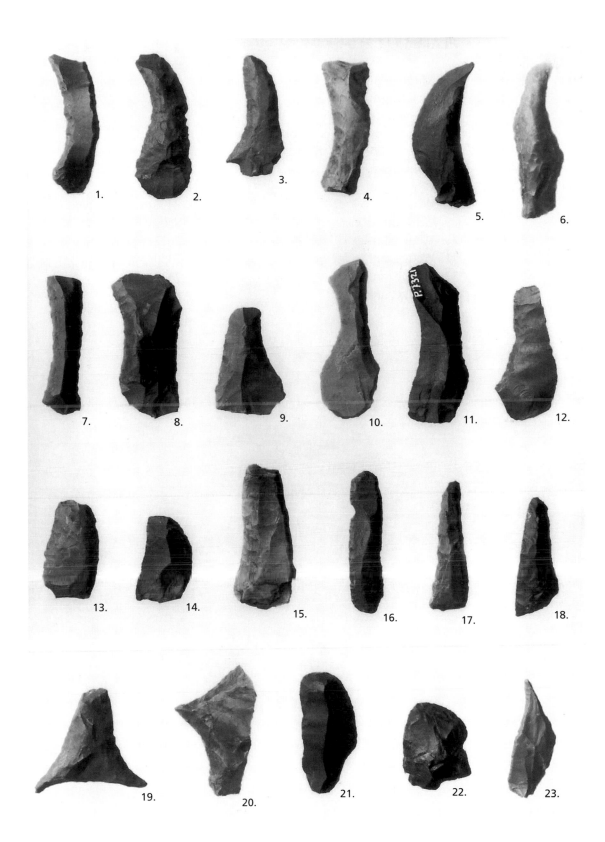

PLATE 17 (1:2)

1.	Mattock head, ivory	7591
2.	Pick fragment (?), bone	7752
3.	Root pick (?), ivory	7328
4.	Handle for mattock or pick?, wood	7960
5.	Whetstone	7182
6.	Whetstone	7573
7.	Whetstone	8341
8.	Whetstone	8496
9.	Grinding stone	8433+8509
10.	Wedge, antler	7612
11.	Wedge, antler	7330
12.	Wedge, antler	7611
13.	Wedge, antler	7678

1.

2.

3.

4.

5.

6.

7.

8.

9.

10.

11.

12.

13.

PLATE 19 (1:3)

1.	Wooden tray	8204
2.	Wooden tray	?
3.	Bowl fragment, wood	8493
4.	Fire drill	7616
5.	Fire drill	7866
6.	Fire drill	7506
7.	Fire drill	8003
8.	Fire drill	7352A
9.	Hearth	7350
10.	Hearth	8466
11.	Hearth	7761
12.	Pyrites	8004

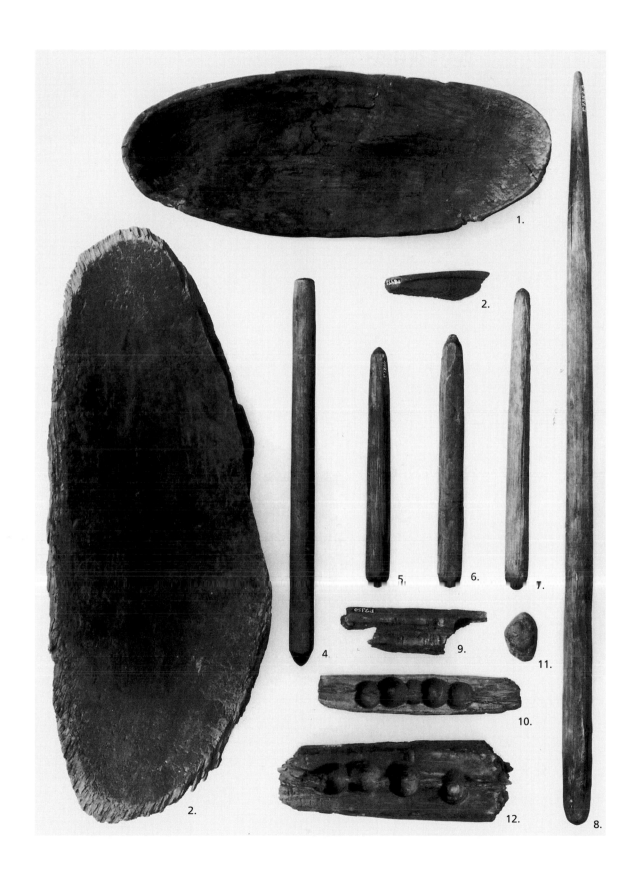

1.

2.

2.

4

5.

6.

7.

8.

9.

10.

11.

12.

PLATE 20 (1:4)

1.	Birch bark, part of container (?)	8471
2.	Birch bark, part of container (?)	8708
3.	Birch bark, sewn	8708
4.	Birch bark, sewn	8164
5.	Birch bark, sewn	8708
6.	Birch bark, sewn	?
7.	Birch bark, sewn, roofing sheet (?)	8494
8.	Birch bark rooled on stick	8515

1.

2.

3.

4.

5.

6.

7.

8.

PLATE 21 (1:2)

1.	Spoon, antler	7237
2.	Spoon, antler	7681
3.	Spoon, ivory	8149
4.	Spoon or ladle, antler	8069
5.	Tubular container, antler	8296+8488
6.	Stone for rubbing paint	7992
7.	Ladle (?), wood	8510
8.	Ladle (?), antler	8356
9.	Ladle (?), wood	8414
10.	Ladle (?), wood	8415
11.	Pumice	?
12.	Ferruginous mineral used for paint (?)	7991
13.	Ferruginous mineral used for paint (?)	8365
14.	Ferruginous mineral used for paint (?)	8365
15.	Piece of four – strand plait	7121
16.	Ring of ?	7240
17.	Coiled basketry, grass	8421
18.	Coiled basketry, grass	8490

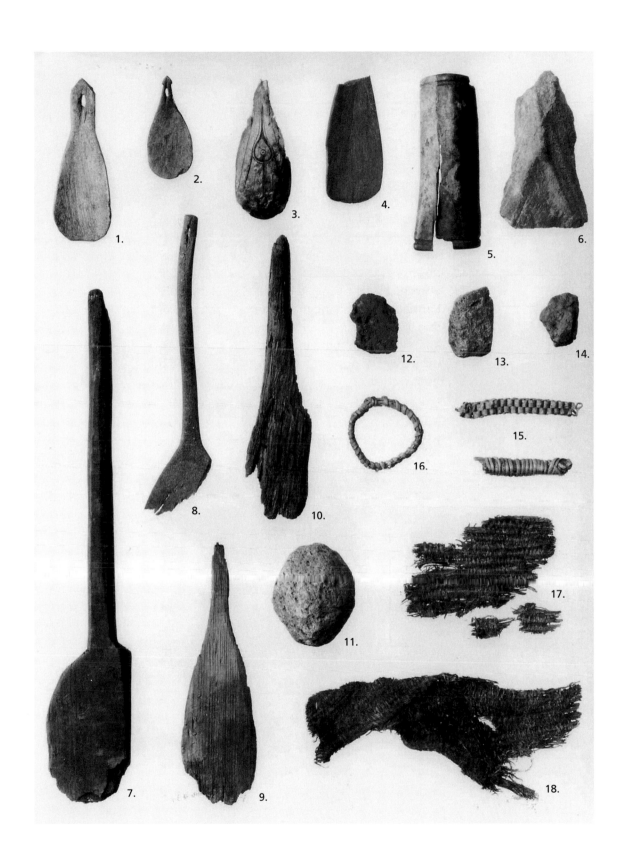

PLATE 22 (1:1)

1. Brow band (?)	7759
2. Brow band (?), antler	8606
3. Brow band (?)	7629
4. Brow band (?), antler	7119
5. Decorated ivory band	8629
6. Snow – goggle fragment, wood	7802
7. Ivory bead	7993
8. Ivory pendant	8569
9. Ivory peg	7994
10. Ivory peg	8745
11. Ivory peg	7808
12. Ivory peg	7995
13. Animal head, carving in antler	7356
14. Carving in ivory	7106A
15. Animal head, carving in antler	8212
16. Implement of uncertain use – type 9	7502
17. Ivory button	8438A

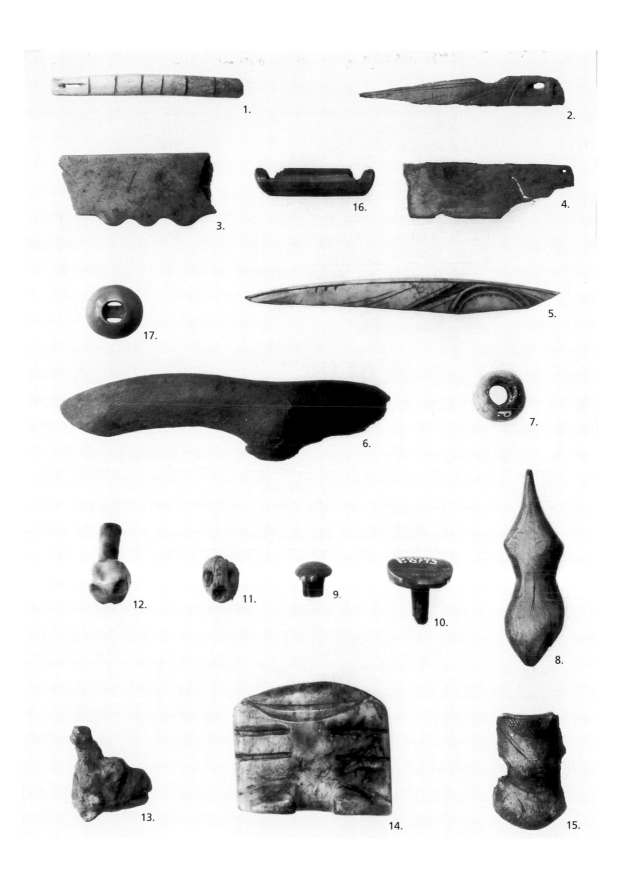

PLATE 23 (2:3)

1. Wood with human features — 7242
2. Wood with human features — 7242
3. Wood with human features — 7242
4. Animal head, wood — 7244
5. Seal figure, ivory — 8745
6. Carving in antler, caribou leg — 8698
7. Wooden object with schematic face — 7959
8. Decorated object, antler — 7354
9. Decorated object, wood — 7688
10. Wooden board with black and red paint — 7869
11. Birch bark with incised decoration — 8245

1.

2.

3.

4.

5.

6.

7.

8.

9.

10.

11.

PLATE 24 (2:3)

1. Snare part of bird bone	7303
2. Snare part of bird bone	7433
3. Snare part of bird bone	7433
4. Snare part of bird bone	8100
5. Snare part of bird bone	8058
6. Implement of uncertain use – type 7, antler	8535
7. Implement of uncertain use – type 7, antler	7503
8. Implement of uncertain use – type 7, antler	7238
9. Implement of uncertain use – type 7, ivory	8605
10. Implement of uncertain use – type 5, ivory	7486
11. Implement of uncertain use – type 5, antler	7333
12. Implement of uncertain use – type 5, ivory	7488
13. Implement of uncertain use – type 5, ivory	7489
14. Implement of uncertain use – type 15, wood	7518
15. Implement of uncertain use – type 15, antler	8627
16. Implement of uncertain use – type 15, antler	7682
17. Implement of uncertain use – type 15, ivory (?)	8321
18. Hook, antler	8487
19. Swivel fragment, antler	8505
20. Implement of uncertain use – type 10, antler	7342
21. Stone sinker	8628
22. Implement of uncertain use – type 12, ivory	8159
23. Bird bone inset in handle	8002

PLATE 25 (1:2)

1.	Snow beater (?)	7632
2.	Snow beater (?)	7916
3.	Snow beater (?)	7508
4.	Snow beater (?)	7372
5.	Handle	7368
6.	Handle	8594
7.	Handle	7134
8.	Handle	7251
9.	Handle	7868
10.	Splice – piece	7378
11.	Splice – piece	7377

PLATE 26 (3:5)

1.	Wooden float?	7507
2.	Wooden float?	7783
3.	Wooden float?	7380
4.	Wooden float?	7637
5.	Wooden float?	7252
6.	Wooden float?	7857
7.	Wooden float?	7782
8.	Wooden float?	7252
9.	Wooden float?	7636
10.	Wooden disc	7379
11.	Wooden disc	7872
12.	Wooden disc	8417
13.	Wooden disc	7509
14.	Amulet box?	7353
15.	Amulet box?	7865
16.	Flat, wooden stick with undulating edges	7820
17.	Flat, wooden stick with undulating edges	8416
18.	Awl – shaped wooden stick	7246
19.	Fragment of unknown object	7638

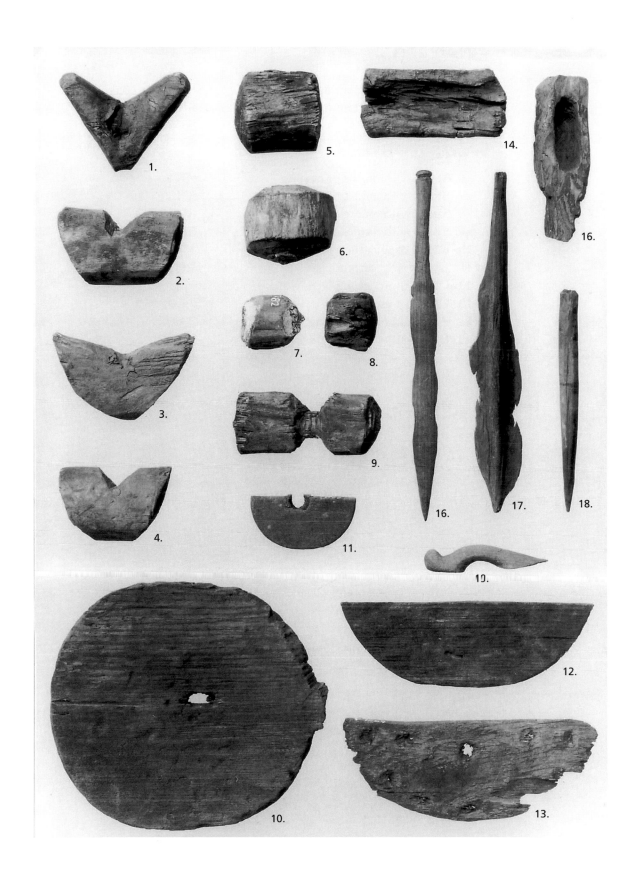

1.

2.

3.

4.

5.

6.

7.

8.

9.

11.

14.

16.

16.

17.

18.

19.

12.

13.

10.

133

PLATE 27 (1:3)

1.	Object of uncertain use	8039
2.	Object of uncertain use	8183
3.	Moulding?	8656
4.	Moulding?	8237
5.	Moulding?	?
6.	Sticks with marks of lashing	7514
7.	Sticks with marks of lashing	8313
8.	Sticks with marks of lashing	8314
9.	Sticks with marks of lashing	8316
10.	Object of uncertain use	8705
11.	Object of uncertain use	7633
12.	Object of uncertain use	7248
13.	Object of uncertain use	7950
14.	Fragment of sled runner?	7366
15.	Fragment of sled runner?	7524

PLATE 28 (1:5)

1.	Side of box ?	7128
2.	Side of box ?	7129
3.	Side of box ?	7829
4.	Board, uncertain use	8238
5.	Board, uncertain use	8513
6.	Side of box ?, painted black	7774
7.	Side of box ?	8391
8.	Object of uncertain use	7253
9.	Wooden stake	8240
10.	Wooden stake	8450
11.	Wooden stake	8586
12.	Wooden stake	7834
13.	Flat stick, use uncertain	7386

PLATE 29 (1:2)

1. Object of uncertain use — 8040
2. Object of uncertain use — 7371
3. Beaver tooth knife handle? — 8206
4. Beaver tooth knife handle? — 8716
5. Stick, use uncertain — 7375
6. Snare part? — 7789
7. Object of uncertain use — 7390
8. Object of uncertain use — 7381
9. Object of uncertain use — 7789
10. Object of uncertain use — 7370
11. Object of uncertain use — 8539
12. Paddle fragment? — 8424
13. Paddle fragment? — 8060
14. Object of uncertain use — 8645
15. Wooden implement of unknown use — 7775
16. Object with four gouged out holes — 7776
17. Toy miniature snowshoe cross piece? — 7524

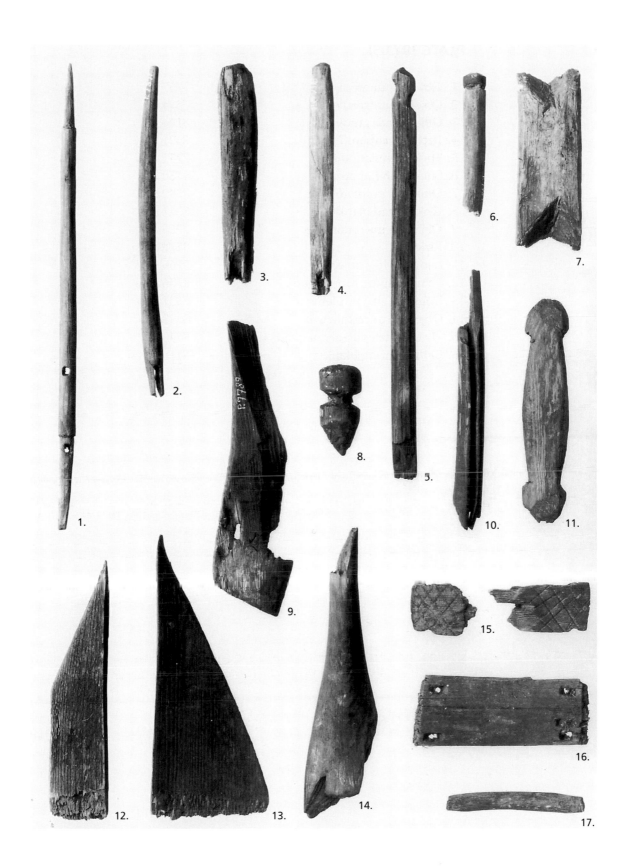

PLATE 30 (3:5)

1.	Object with groove	7757
2.	Object with groove	7504
3.	Object with groove	8144
4.	Part of weapon (?)	7501
5.	Stick with flat point	7751
6.	Stick with flat point	8430
7.	Double – pointed stick	8142
8.	Arrowhead blank (?)	8347
9.	Object of uncertain use	7953
10.	Ring	8172
11.	Laddle – like object	7766
12.	Salmon spear prong blank (?)	7756
13.	Dagger – like implement	7331
14.	Object of uncertain use	8699
15.	Object related to arrowheads (?)	8740
16.	Barbed prong blank	8118

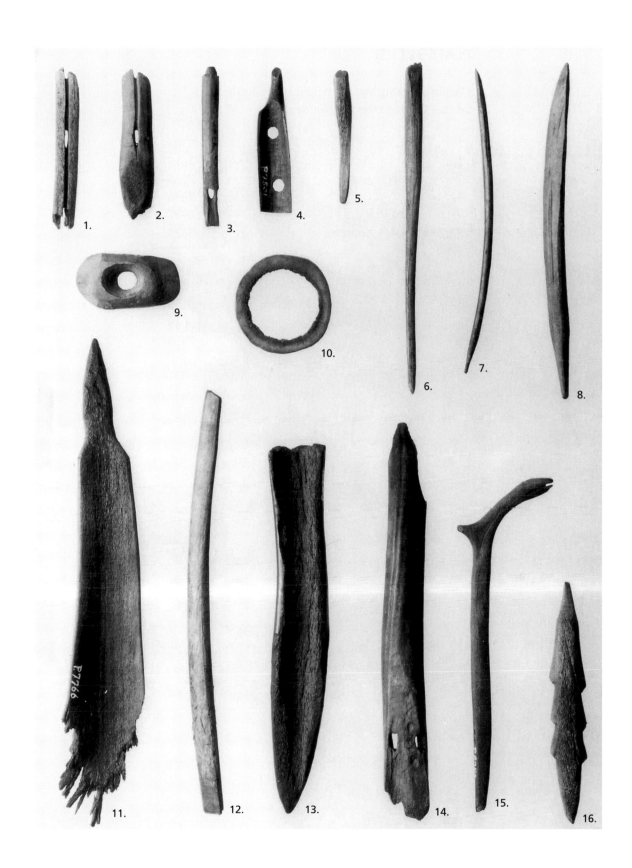

PLATE 31 (3:5)

(Various examples of worked ivory, antler and bone. Not described by Larsen)

1.	7388
2.	7617
3.	7264
4.	7388
5.	7967
6.	8323
7.	7700
8.	7389
9.	7701
10.	8175
11.	7648
12.	7956

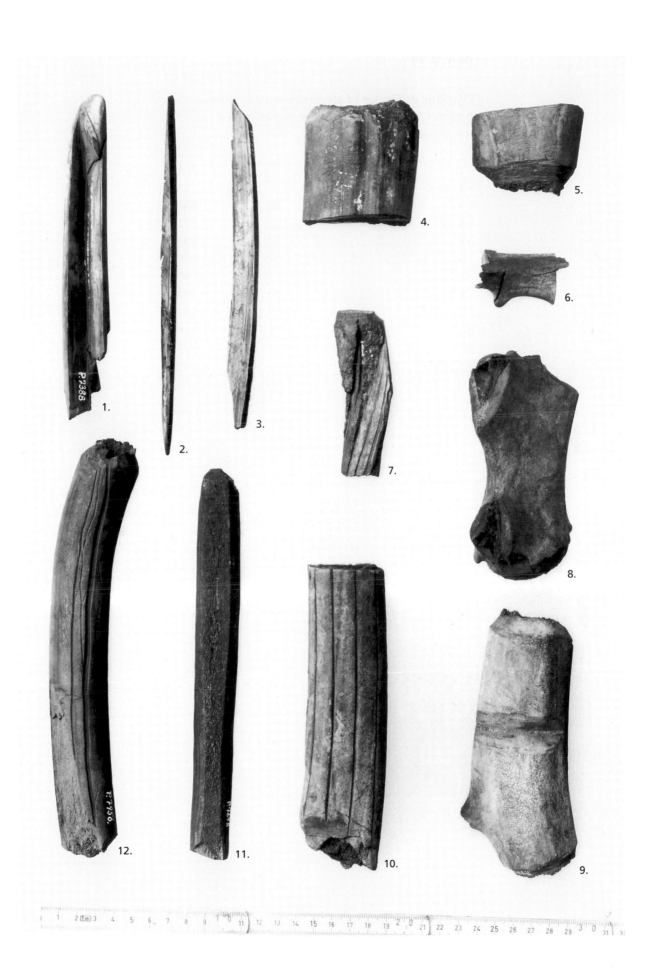

PLATE 32

(Various examples of objects of willow – root and baleen (?), including an amulet (8037). Not described by Larsen).

1.	8519
2.	?
3.	8519
4.	8713
5.	7947
6.	8388
7.	8498
8.	7882
9.	7946
10.	8103
11.	7777
12.	8037

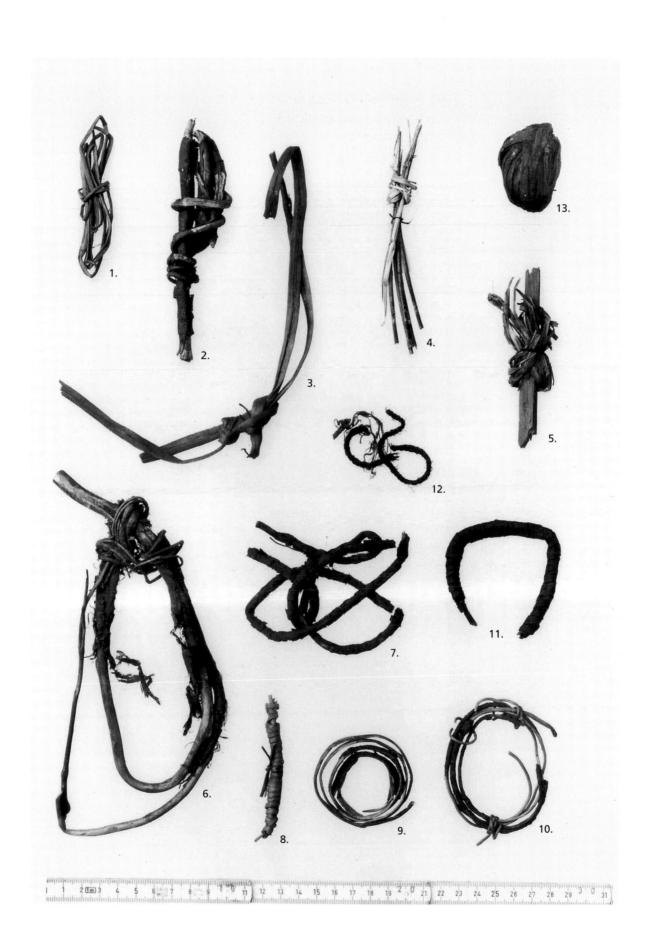